W9-CGX-843

Performance Notes by Greg P. Herriges

ISBN 1-4234-0776-8

HAL•LEONARD® CORPORATION

7777 W. BLUEMOUND RD. P.O. BOX 13819 MILWAUKEE, WI 53213

Visit Hal Leonard Online at
www.halleonard.com

Table of Contents

Introduction 4

    About This Book...4

    How to Use This Book...4

    Icons Used in This Book 5

Performance Notes...7

    Ain't Talkin' 'Bout Love..7

    All Right Now..7

    Born to Be Wild..8

    The Boys Are Back in Town 9

    Brown Eyed Girl 9

    Drive My Car...10

    Fun, Fun, Fun 10

    Hey Joe...11

    Hit Me With Your Best Shot..12

    I Want You to Want Me 12

    Message in a Bottle 13

    Mississippi Queen...13

    Money for Nothing..14

    Oh, Pretty Woman...15

    Proud Mary...15

    Rebel, Rebel..16

    Refugee...16

    Rock and Roll All Nite 17

    R.O.C.K. in the U.S.A. (A Salute to 60's Rock)..17

    Rock This Town 18

    Rock'n Me 19

    Rocky Mountain Way...19

    Shattered...20

    Smoke on the Water 20

    Summer of '69..21

    Sunshine of Your Love 21

    Sweet Home Alabama..22

    Takin' Care of Business...23

    Tush..23

    Walk Don't Run...24

    Walk This Way 25

    What I Like About You 25

    Wild Thing...26

    Won't Get Fooled Again...26

    You Give Love a Bad Name..27

Music..*28*

    Ain't Talkin' 'Bout Love...28

    All Right Now...37

    Born to Be Wild...46

    The Boys Are Back in Town 50

    Brown Eyed Girl..56

    Drive My Car...64

    Fun, Fun, Fun...68

    Hey Joe..75

    Hit Me With Your Best Shot...83

    I Want You to Want Me 89

    Message in a Bottle 97

    Mississippi Queen...102

    Money for Nothing...108

    Oh, Pretty Woman...115

    Proud Mary..121

    Rebel, Rebel..126

    Refugee..132

    Rock and Roll All Nite 138

    R.O.C.K. in the U.S.A. (A Salute to 60's Rock) 143

    Rock This Town 150

    Rock'n Me 160

    Rocky Mountain Way...166

    Shattered...172

    Smoke on the Water 179

    Summer of '69...185

    Sunshine of Your Love 193

    Sweet Home Alabama...198

    Takin' Care of Business 207

    Tush...215

    Walk Don't Run...220

    Walk This Way...223

    What I Like About You 230

    Wild Thing..235

    Won't Get Fooled Again...240

    You Give Love a Bad Name..248

Guitar Notation Legend...*254*

Chord Chart..*256*

Introduction

*W*elcome to *Rock Guitar Songs For Dummies!* Everything you need to play some of the greatest and most popular songs in rock music is here, including note-for-note transcriptions of the songs, and performance notes that will help you through them — without the need for a music degree to understand the terms.

About This Book

The music in this book is in standard notation and *tablature* (also known as *tab*) — which is a diagram of the guitar strings with numbers that tell you what *frets* to play. I assume you know a little something about reading tab or music, but a Guitar Notation Legend in the back of the book can help translate all those strange words, symbols, and hieroglyphs that are the written language of guitar. I also assume that you know a little bit about the guitar itself — like how to hold it, where the neck and frets are, how to tune it, basic chord strumming, and how to look cool while doing it. If you need a refresher course on rock guitar basics, please check out *Rock Guitar For Dummies*, by Jon Chappell and Carl Verheyen (Wiley).

Also included in the back is a chart of common chords, so (for my own sake) I don't have to list them for every song. This is handy, because where a line of tablature gives you fret numbers, a chord diagram shows you the visual *shape* of the chord and which fingers to use.

New concepts are introduced as they appear, and referred back to when necessary. So you can skip around the book and pick out your favorite songs first, without missing out on essential information.

How to Use This Book

For every song, I give you a brief intro with a little background on the artist (in case you're not already a rock trivia god), followed by the essential bits you need to learn the song:

- A run-down of the parts you need to know, not including those parts that are clones of other sections of the song.

- A breakdown of some of the special techniques you need to play the song — the trade secrets you won't see on the sheet music.

- When necessary, some info you need to navigate the sheet music (such as codas, repeats, and so on.)

Of course, you may already know a lot of this stuff, so feel free to skip it as you choose — unless you find the writing especially witty, entertaining, and eloquent (yeah, right). The best strategy is always to go through the song and find all the main chords and their positions (the chord chart at the back can help), then try working in all the licks and tricks. Also, if you have access to the original recordings of the songs, listening to them as you practice will help tremendously.

Your other left

No two guitarists are the same, and some of the greatest ones happen to play left-handed — so forgive your author/teacher for sometimes referring to the picking hand as "right" and the fretting hand as "left." I avoid these conventions as much as possible, but sometimes there's no better way to say it.

Down is up

When I talk about low and high strings, I'm talking pitchwise, in terms of what you hear, not what you see. Your low E string, for example, is the string on "top," the fattest one with the lowest sound. The high E string is the skinny one on the "bottom," and so on. I'll try to be as clear as possible on whether I'm talking about sound or sight.

Here are some common guitar terms discussed throughout the book:

- ✔ **Barre chords** (chords in which one finger holds down two or more strings at once)
- ✔ **Box** (the physical shape formed by common note patterns played on the fretboard; **blues box** is another common way to describe the same concept)
- ✔ **Open strings** (strings played in **open position**, without a finger on the fretboard)
- ✔ **Riffs** (repeating bits of music that are noteworthy enough to mention) and **licks** (common lead guitar tricks)
- ✔ **Strumming** (using a guitar pick to "fling" across the strings, often in a pattern of **downstrokes** — strumming down toward the earth — and **upstrokes** toward the sky)
- ✔ **Other terms** that are explained in the Guitar Notation Legend. In the performance notes, when you see an unfamiliar word in *italics*, that's your cue to consult the back of the book.

Icons Used in This Book

In the margins of this book are several little icons that will help make your life easier:

A reason to stop and review advice that can prevent damage to your fingers, ears, guitar, or ego.

Optional parts, like solos, that may be too challenging for many guitarists, but are discussed anyway for the learned and/or ambitious "champion" players among you. In these discussions I'll have to throw lots of strange terms at you, all of which can be found in the Guitar Notation Legend.

Details (like tunings and special techniques) that you need to know, and will probably need again in the future.

Notes about specific musical concepts that are relevant but confusing to the layperson. Sometimes it's just something I notice that's especially cool to musicians!

Shortcuts and suggested ways to get through some of the difficult bits without tangling your fingers.

Performance Notes

Ain't Talkin' 'Bout Love (page 28)

What book on rock guitar would be complete without reference to the man who popularized two-handed tapping and striped guitars? Eddie Van Halen took some very special guitar techniques and went gonzo with them, turning rock guitar into a feast for the fingers and setting the standards for a generation of flash gods. "Ain't Talkin' 'Bout Love" was on the first, self-titled 1978 album of Van Halen the band (named after Eddie and his equally gonzo drummer brother, Alex).

Rock tuning

This song is in an alternative standard tuning used by great rock guitarists who like to make life difficult for guitar teachers. Each string is tuned down a half step lower than in standard tuning, in order to make it easier to bend strings and belt out high vocals. Open strings, low to high, are Eb–Ab–Db–Gb–Bb–Eb, but you don't need to tune down unless you plan to play with the original recording.

Palm muting 101

How nice of Mr. Ed to give you the perfect introduction to *palm muting* in the intro riff. Put the edge of your right palm where the strings meet the bridge of the guitar, and press your palm down lightly while you pick the notes. You want to hear a "chunk" sound as you palm mute. If you're not hearing it, try moving your hand further inward, or press the edge of your palm down harder — but not too hard, or you might raise the pitch of the notes you're playing. Palm muting is abbreviated as "P.M." in the music.

From the intro on, all parts are variations on the same chord pattern (basically Am–G), with lots of special techniques: *pinch harmonics, vibrato,* vibrato bar *dips,* string *bends, pick scrapes, slides,* "dive bombs," *harmonics,* and so on. After Sir Edward came along, new notation had to be made up to symbolize some of these things! Consult the Guitar Notation Legend for details.

Shred like Ed

Most of the guitar solo is played with an upper *drone* string — one note that keeps ringing while others move. While you play the moving notes on the B string (second from bottom), it's important to keep your fretting finger out of the way of the open high E. When you get to the top of the riff, do the quick licks by picking the B string once, *hammering-on* three frets higher, *pulling-off,* then picking the note on the G string — all in quick succession. The Guitar Notation Legend describes *hammer-ons* and *pull-offs* as well.

If the techniques in this song are intimidating, don't fret — you can move on to some less-gonzo songs that introduce the same techniques, then come back to this one with a more seasoned perspective. Check out "All Right Now" for more on *bending* and "Smoke on the Water" for some vibrato bar techniques.

All Right Now (page 37)

Here's a tale of a dude trying to talk a lady into a bit of fun. I don't know the outcome, but I know the song was a huge success for the pioneering British blues-rock band Free, as was the 1970 album *Fire and Water* from which it came. The late guitarist Paul Kossoff shows his restrained but expressive playing style on this classic-rock radio staple song.

Power chords

A chord labeled with a "5" after it is known as a *power chord* (or simply a "five" chord), which only contains two notes, the 1st and the 5th (and any repeated octaves of both), and is missing the all-important 3rd — the note that usually determines the mood: major or minor, happy or sad. Without that note, you get a powerful sound that expresses a third emotion, known as "rock."

"All Right Now" starts with the coolest power chord ever: an A5 played with a *partial* barre. Put your first finger flat over the second-fret strings, and stretch your pinky over the fifth fret on the bottom two strings. Then you can keep your first finger in place for the next chord! The same pattern plays out until the chorus, which is built mostly on two-note power chords.

Bending 101

Both guitar solos are full of bluesy string *bends* of all kinds. The first type of *bend* you'll see is a quarter step; pull the string slightly *downward* after you pick it (a little more pulling will make it a half step). A bend of a whole step or more (as in the third bar of the first guitar solo) should be pushed *upward*. You want the note to sound like it's moving up two frets, so push hard enough to make that happen. (You can wrap your thumb around the top of the neck to give more leverage.) See the Guitar Notation Legend for other soloing techniques.

In the first guitar solo, you'll also notice a two-and-a-half-step bend — try this only if your strings are light and your hands are strong! You may break a string, so protect yourself with full body armor.

D.S. *(Dal Segno)* **al Coda** means "from the sign to the tail." For an English translation, see the Guitar Notation Legend. This song has two codas, played in sequence.

Born to Be Wild *(page 46)*

Steppenwolf, the Canadian/U.S. band named after a Hermann Hesse novel, were the early psychedelic masters of macho *power chords* (see "All Right Now"). This, the song that coined the term "heavy metal," was on the band's self-titled 1968 debut album, and later was used in the *Easy Rider* soundtrack. It has since become a theme song for bikers (and biker wannabes) everywhere. Guitarist Michael Monarch and singer John Kay wield the thunderous axes.

Blues barre

The song starts with a full E barre chord, in which one finger (preferably the ring finger) covers three strings at once. Then comes a blues move, with the pinky extending to hit higher notes on the D string. Luckily, you can lift up the barring finger while you make this stretch. Try moving your middle finger to fret 9 (if it cooperates) — then it's easier to play the next couple of notes.

The verse has a repeated variation on that riff, with *palm muting* (see "Ain't Talkin' 'Bout Love") in between. Play the muted part with all downstrokes. The pre-chorus has more full barre chords and fills with *bending* (see "All Right Now"). As a general rule, bend upward (toward the sky) on the bottom three (skinnier) strings, and downward (toward the earth) on the top three (fatter) strings. The boxes at the bottom of the page show different fills that get used in different verses — they're all variations on the same move.

The Jimi Hendrix chord

If you're comfortable with lots of barre chords, the rest of the song is a piece of cake. Notice the E7♯9 chord during the organ solo — not a barre, but a slightly jazzy, Hendrix-ey chord — repeated with a quick "down, down–up" strum and string *muffling* (see the Guitar Notation Legend) in between. The following single-note line can be played with one finger, if you like!

The Boys Are Back in Town (page 50)

Dublin, Ireland's Thin Lizzy was one of the first rock groups to use double-lead guitar harmony — a technique made trendy by many later bands with more hairspray and tighter trousers. Lizzy was also a breeding ground for many notable guitarists over the years. From the 1976 album *Jailbreak*, "The Boys Are Back in Town" features the riffing of Scott Gorham and Brian Robertson, in addition to singer/bassist/guitarist Phil Lynott.

Rock tuning

If you want to play this song along with the original recording, tune your guitar down one half step below standard. (Check "Ain't Talkin' 'Bout Love" for an explanation of "rock tuning" and why it rocks.)

Swing it!

When you play with a *shuffle* (or *swing*) *feel,* a pair of eighth notes turns into something completely different (see the tempo indicator at the start of the song). But don't sweat the notation; just think of it as playing more like a heartbeat. Unless you're a robot, your heart doesn't beat in straight eighth notes; it has a long beat and a short beat. When you strum or pick with a shuffle feel, the downstroke is usually longer than the upstroke. It's a natural feel that's big in jazz and blues, but used universally.

Irish jazz-rock?

The intro, basically the same as the chorus, has *power chords* (see "All Right Now") with a *palm-muted* fill (see "Ain't Talkin' 'Bout Love") in between. But wait — has the verse morphed into a different tune? This progression of barre chords is straight out of jazz, a great contrast to the straight-up chorus. Learn the chords first, then play through it.

Triple your pleasure

The chorus end has a mini guitar solo that makes full use of *hammer-ons*, *vibrato*, and *triplets* — not three identical siblings, but three notes grouped in the space of four, or two, or one. You can learn to feel triplets by reciting, "trip–uh–let, trip–uh–let," over a four-count. You can do this with the last measure of the chorus solo, which is broken up into six notes. You'll also see triplets in other sections of the song; listen, count, and tap along with the rhythms to get a feel for the triplets.

The interlude is a tasteful and spacious guitar solo (with *slides*), followed by more of that catchy chorus riff. Check out the Guitar Notation Legend to learn about *hammer-ons*, *vibrato*, and *slides*.

Brown Eyed Girl (page 56)

From the other side of Ireland, Belfast native Van Morrison created and popularized the jazz/blues/pop/folk style sometimes referred to as "Celtic Soul." His biggest hit, "Brown Eyed Girl," was on his 1967 solo debut album with the way-groovy title *Blowin' Your Mind!*

Hybrid picking

The Afropop-sounding intro riff, and much of the rest of the song, is played "w/ pick & fingers" — also known as *hybrid picking*. When you see two notes that are more than one string apart, play the lower note with your pick while your middle finger plucks the higher note. Get used to this technique if you can — you'll need it later.

Dyads

What you're playing in the intro and later on in the song are called *dyads* — two-note chords — that follow the G major scale. There are certain shapes of dyads that can be used to climb up and down the whole neck in certain keys. For now, follow the tab, and you may see a pattern developing!

Strumming

The verse is strummed (in a pattern like "down, down–up, up–down–up") with basic chords, which means that your picking hand is in a constant up-and-down motion, but not hitting the strings every time. To keep a steady rhythm, your hand should continue playing "ghost strums" (strums that make no contact with the strings) during the pauses in the strumming pattern.

The end of the verse calls for more hybrid picking — know the chords first, then try the picking. Consider all of these moves as chord changes; the fingers you use to move the notes around depend on the chord positions. You only absolutely need that picking middle finger when you pick two notes at a time — otherwise, you can use the pick only.

The chorus features straight strumming of the same chord pattern as the verse, but you play the chords in a different position: at fret 3, in *closed position* — without any open strings.

Drive My Car (page 64)

One of the first songs to use the lyrical innovation, "beep, beep, mm, beep, beep," "Drive My Car" first appeared on the UK version of the 1965 Beatles album *Rubber Soul*. Speaking of soul, that's the kind of music this tune emulates in its arrangement and guitar playing. The late lead guitarist George Harrison got slightly funky on this one.

Time warp

The opening riff is played with *slides*, a half-step downward *bend*, and *double stops* (two notes played together on adjacent strings), over a strange pair of measures — one 4/4 and the next 9/8! (This measure has nine beats, and an eighth note gets one beat.) This is just the transcriber's way of writing out what can't be fit into an even-numbered box, and it's better felt than counted. The rest of the song is in a nice, even 4/4. Check out the Guitar Notation Legend for more on *slides* and *bends*.

Bass riffin'

Most of this song is guitar playing along with the bass in unison. This combination makes for a driving sound that was big in soul music at the time, and it gives you a taste of what life is like for the bass player — not as easy as you might think! The riff involves a lot of shifting and sliding, but the verse is just one pattern repeated in different positions. The chorus goes elsewhere; just follow the notes and you'll see the patterns that go with each chord.

Finger jam

You're normally taught to use one finger per fret when soloing. Kindly disregard that rule for this guitar solo, which could be quite awkward if played by the rules. Start by bending the D string *downward* with your first finger, then use your middle finger on fret 12. This move enables you to reach over with the ring finger for the following bend (push *upward* this time). Then place your first finger on fret 12 while the middle finger below it plays the half-step *pre-bend* — quickly pull the G string downward before you pick it, then pick and release. The next half-step bend is likewise downward, and everything repeats. After the slides comes a one-and-a-half-step upward bend — watch for flying strings!

Fun, Fun, Fun (page 68)

"Fun, Fun, Fun" is an automotive love song, one of many odes to hot rods, girls, and surfin' from California's perpetual teenagers, the Beach Boys. This Top 10 hit was from their fifth album, *Shut Down Volume 2* (1964). Lead guitarist Carl Wilson, the youngest of the Brothers Wilson, gives you his best Chuck Berry-isms.

Rock tuning

You can rock without "rock tuning," but if you want to play this song along with the original recording, tune your guitar down one half step below standard. (Check "Ain't Talkin' 'Bout Love" for an explanation of this tuning.)

The beach box

The first Chuck Berry-ism comes in the intro. When playing in the key of E, you can use the box shape formed between frets 12 and 15 to solo in the early rock 'n' roll style. This solo is built on *double stops* (two notes played together on adjacent strings), *hammer-ons*, and a kind of *unison bend* — push the G string up a step on fret 14, stop it there, and hit the same note on the B string, fret 12. Repeat. Repeat again. And again. Fun, isn't it? A half-step *bend* of two strings comes later; pull both strings downward with one finger.

The verse is played mostly in two-finger *power chords* (see "All Right Now"), *palm muted* (a technique explained in "Ain't Talkin' 'Bout Love") with some blues-style rocking. When the singer pauses on the A chord, rock back and forth between the second and fourth fret while keeping the A string going underneath. You do the same on the B chord, but here you have to keep the chord fretted while stretching your pinky to hit the sixth fret. All chords in this song are based on the same two-finger shape, just moved around the fretboard.

Guitar solo

The main guitar solo doesn't stay in one box like the intro; it actually moves around to a few different boxes depending on the chords over which you're playing the solo. You can pull downward with one finger on both strings for those half-step bends, and push upward on the whole-step bend. Notice the *slide* when you move up to fret 14 for the B chord. Check the Guitar Notation Legend for information on *hammer-ons* and *slides*.

Hey Joe *(page 75)*

Where you goin' with that charred Stratocaster in your hand? This fiery treatment of "Hey Joe" became the definitive rock version of a 1960s folk classic, a song that was covered by everyone from the Surfaris to Cher. The Jimi Hendrix Experience version was from their 1967 debut album, *Are You Experienced?* Indeed, you may need a little experience to play everything in this song, but you can get the basics here.

The song opens with licks based around an E chord. The ultimate Hendrix lick is in measure 3: Hold your first finger on fret 7, and *hammer on* fret 9 with your ring finger, picking the upper chord between each hammer. Watch for the same sort of thing throughout the song.

Hendrix 101

Jimi's free-form guitar style is hard to teach in words. Basically, he takes the main chord progression and fills all over it, never the same way twice. Check out the basic chords first: The C is a barre (the ring finger covers three strings on fret 5), and the G is played with the thumb wrapped around the guitar neck on the E string! Try it this way, but try it also with a full barre (first finger over all six strings) and do what works for you. D is a barre, and A and E are standard. Around these chords he works in *hammer-ons*, *slides*, *bends*, *muffled* strings, and *triplets* (see "The Boys Are Back in Town" for an explanation of triplets).

Psychedelic blues

Most of the guitar solo is played in a box position between frets 12 and 15. It's very blues-based, and in fact contains the same licks you see in "Fun, Fun, Fun" — the difference is in the feel. There's *bending with vibrato* — push the string up and shake it while holding it up, bent. There are *unison bends*, *slides*, and *double stops* (two notes played together on adjacent strings), all played very smoothly.

One technique you may not have seen yet: In the last verse, after the line "Mexico way," there's a *trill*, with one note held on fret 2 while you repeatedly *hammer-on* and *pull-off* on fret 4 with lightning speed. Do so, and make Mr. Hendrix proud! If you are confused by any of the terms used here, be sure to consult the Guitar Notation Legend.

Hit Me With Your Best Shot (page 83)

If every decade has a rock diva, Pat Benatar must be it for the '80s. Her operatic rock vocals and tough lyrics, mixed with the bluesy rock abandon of husband/guitarist Neil Geraldo, made for some genuine pop-rock chutzpah in an age with lots of plastic in it. This 1980 Top 10 hit was one of many from the album *Crimes of Passion*.

Chords

The song is built mostly on *second-position* barre chords, in which the bottom note is on the A string, and one finger (usually) covers the next three strings. Just move the shape around to different frets, but notice that the C♯m chord is a different shape on the same strings. When you *palm mute* in the verse, gradually let up on the pressure so that the chord slowly opens up and gets louder. See "Ain't Talkin' 'Bout Love" for more on *palm muting*.

Hit me with your best solo

The guitar solo is full of chaotic fun, like the opening *arpeggio* (a chord played one note at a time), best played with a *sweep-picking* technique: all downstrokes across three strings. You get a chance to practice a lot of *hammering* and *pulling* over an open B string (like a moving *trill*), *vibrato*, string *damping*, and *bending* — remember that for a whole-step bend, you want the *bent* note to sound like a fretted note two frets higher; compare the two to get it on pitch. After *sliding* around the neck, there's a whole-step *pre-bend* that you need to push up before you pick it. See the Guitar Notation Legend for more on these techniques.

The last verse is palm muted again, and those notes are just chord tones; start by holding your first finger on the D string, fret 2; ring finger on the G string, fret 4; and pinky on the B string, fret 5. Now you're in position to play the verse by moving and lifting off fingers from that position.

Finally, when you play the quarter-step bends that end the song, put your pick way back where the strings meet the guitar's bridge — that will create the twangy cowboy sound that's called for.

I Want You to Want Me (page 89)

Look up the definition of "power pop," and you'll see a picture of Cheap Trick. The Illinois band hit the big time with the 1978 live album *At Budokan*, which contained the popular version of "I Want You to Want Me" (a less rockin' version of the song had been on their 1977 album *In Color*). Rick Nielsen, the self-proclaimed "Pee-Wee Herman of rock 'n' roll," gives you the classic lead licks, backed up by singer/guitarist Robin Zander.

A different kind of shuffle

My notes for "The Boys Are Back in Town" explain the concepts of *swing* or *shuffle feel*. Here's a bouncy *double-time shuffle*, in which the sixteenth notes are displaced into a long beat and a short beat. Just think of it as a fast heartbeat.

The licks come in right off the bat, with a *bent* note underneath a held note. Make sure that your *bend* is a precise whole step, and the other note is not *bent* — or else your neighbors may complain about the tortured animal sounds coming from your room. See "All Right Now" for more on *bending*.

Play the lower notes in the chorus with a *palm mute* (see "Ain't Talkin' 'Bout Love"), but pick up the palm to do a quick upstroke on the upper chords. When you start filling later, make sure that your bends are on pitch. Most are whole-step bends, so the bent note sounds like a note two frets higher than the starting point.

Swinging sextuplets

At the end of the chorus is a quick pair of *sextuplets* — groups of six rhythmically identical notes, not siblings. Here they're sets of *pull-offs*, played by picking one note, pulling it off to a note two frets below, then pulling that one off to an open string. Repeating in another position, then on another string, yields one of the coolest riffs ever. See the Guitar Notation Legend for more on *pull-offs*.

The pre-chorus has some blues rocking and partial barre chords, and the next chorus involves more of the same filling tricks you saw earlier. Then come two solos, where you need to bend a string under a held note again — but this time, pick the notes separately. Rick uses a lot of *dyads* and *double stops*, both of which are partial chords that move around the neck. When you fret these partial chords, you'll notice that the notes form into a couple shapes that you play in different places on the fretboard.

Message in a Bottle (page 97)

The Police grew out of the British punk/new wave scene in the late 1970s to become one of the most successful pop bands of the '80s. Their 1979 second album, *Regatta de Blanc* ("white reggae"), showcased the developing sound of Andy Summers, whose tasteful jazz-influenced playing and equally tasteful guitar sounds would create trends in the decade to come and beyond.

Finger suggestions

Stretch out your fretting fingers! "Message in a Bottle" is played with sus2 chords. You need three fingers — ideally index, middle, and pinky — each playing two frets away from the next for these sus2 shapes. It's just one chord shape moved around to different frets, with a pinky slide at the end of the pattern. This pattern repeats for a while, so get used to the positioning.

Play the *power chords* (see "All Right Now") in the pre-chorus with all downstrokes and no *palm muting* (see "Ain't Talkin' 'Bout Love"), so it's driving and open (in the style of the punk-rock scene that spawned the Police). Contrast that rhythm with the chorus, which is strummed tastefully in full barre chords. "Fling" your pick slowly across the strings, from low E to high E, for every chord. (Notice the jazzy F♯m that ends the section.) Then you're ready to jump back into the busy verse.

The Police sound

Guitar sounds are especially important in a song and style like this. For "Message in a Bottle," you need to add just a touch of distortion to the sound of your guitar, which in a perfect world is a Fender Strat or Telecaster. In addition, a chorus effect, set to a slow rate and medium intensity, adds the perfect shimmer.

Mississippi Queen (page 102)

The mountainous Leslie West was frontman and lead guitarist for the influential blues-rock band Mountain. In addition to being a spelling lesson, "Mississippi Queen" is a driving tune from the band's second album, *Climbing!* (1970). West's precise riffing, *power chords* (see "All Right Now"), and gritty voice help give this song its huge, proto-metal sound.

Pick 'n' shake

Play the opening riff (and all riffs) with *alternate picking*, "down–up–down–up," and add *vibrato* on the last note before *sliding* down the string (see the Guitar Notation Legend for more on *vibrato* and *slides*). Vibrato style is important throughout this song. Practice with a smooth shake of the wrist, not a muscle spasm of the entire arm. You will develop a better feel for vibrato over time, but you want to avoid bad habits early on.

Riff + power chord = rock

Throughout the song are *bent* strings with held notes above — be precise, or neighborhood dogs may start howling. At the start of the chorus is a quick *pull-off* and vibrato, then slide down — pure blues (in the style of B.B. King). Between the sliding power chords are *muffled* strums and riffs with half-step bends (pull the string downward slightly after you pick it). Notice that the same licks move to different strings as the chords change.

The guitar solo continues the themes of the intro and verse, with bonus frills like a *two-string bend* — pull this downward. Later you see *held bends* at fret 19; push the string up, hold it there, pick it again, and repeat.

Bend 'n' shake

Bending with vibrato is an acquired skill, requiring you to shake the string while it's pushed up. Try it slowly: Push the string up a step, let it drop just a tiny bit, and push it back up again. Repeat, and work on speeding it up until your hand works like a human spring. (Extra Tip: wrapping your thumb around the neck gives you extra leverage.) Consult the Guitar Notation Legend for help in deciphering the many "guitarisms" in this song.

Money for Nothing (page 108)

Throw away your pick! Guitarist and Scotsman Mark Knopfler's one-of-a-kind guitar style, using good old flesh on strings, drove the sound of Dire Straits. This #2 hit from their fifth album, *Brothers in Arms* (1985), was a huge MTV-era statement and success.

Play this with your picking-hand thumb, index, and middle fingers. The song is mostly just plucked *power chords* (see "All Right Now"), some of them *slid* and *hammered* from one position to the next, and the arrangement is casual. For the first G5 chord, lay your index finger over the strings on fret 5, so you can easily lift off the seventh-fret note for the chord change.

Pops and clicks

The occasional *harmonics* are just incidental "pops" with the thumb, while a left-hand finger touches the D string lightly over fret 5. Wherever you see "dead" or *muffled* notes, just flick the *muffled* strings with the back of your right-hand fingernail.

Keep plucking over the chorus, until the phrase "we gotta move these color TVs" — there, strum with your thumb or fingernail to add some momentum. Then it's back to plucking for verse 2, which ends with a *pull-off*; barre both strings with the middle finger, *pull off* to the index, then play open. Check out the Guitar Notation Legend for help with any of these techniques.

Knopfler improvises and throws in lots of variations throughout this song, and the operative word is *subtlety*. Never play too fast or too hard, and stay in the moderate groove of the song.

The Strait sound

Knopfler used some kind of pickup phase reversal to get that nasal guitar tone, but you can get close to it with a couple of effects: smooth distortion, and a wah-wah pedal balanced right around the midpoint between the "w" and the "ah." If you don't have a wah, try cranking the midrange all the way up on your amplifier, and turning your guitar's tone knob down.

Oh, Pretty Woman (page 115)

The late Roy Orbison, singer/songwriter extraordinaire, had a #1 hit in 1964 with this song, which sold more records in its first ten days than any other 45 rpm single in history! Also featured on the 1965 album *Orbisongs*, "Oh, Pretty Woman" was later covered by Van Halen and many others, and the song's influence can be heard everywhere from the Beatles to Devo!

Time shift

Don't sweat the changing time signatures in this song; they're just a way to notate what comes naturally. Two measures of 6/4 time in the intro simply give an extra pair of beats for a short pause. The same is true of the 2/4 measure later in the verse; it's used to accommodate the lyrics.

Fingers never forget

The classic opening riff can be played with a one-finger-per-string approach. Your first finger takes fret 2, ring on fret 4, and pinky on 5. It's a great exercise for dexterity and what is called "finger memory." Play in any picking pattern you choose.

The verse is strummed in a pattern like "down, down–up, up–down–up." Remember that for every pause in the strumming, it's best to play "ghost strums" as if your hand is playing straight eighth notes. The F♯m is the only full barre chord throughout the song.

Harmonic convergence

The bridge continues with the same strum pattern in a different key. Note that the A chord is minor until the line, "with me . . . " where it becomes major, and the song *modulates* (changes key) back from C to the original A. Confused? Just know that all this technical talk can be summed up in very common musical term: cool.

Proud Mary (page 121)

This signature song by Creedence Clearwater Revival, from their 1969 album *Bayou Country*, was written by singer/lead guitarist John Fogerty and backed up on rhythm by his brother Tom. Creedence's style blended elements of rock 'n' roll, blues, gospel, and soul into a fine gumbo of '60s hits. "Proud Mary" has their typical down-home Louisiana feel, plus a guitar solo that's straight out of Memphis soul.

Strumming upstream

The catchy intro is strummed, and makes great use of upstrokes. The second chord falls on "beat 2½," and the rests between upstrokes are just slaps of the picking hand on the strings. The strum pattern through the verse is "down–up–x–up–down–up–x–up–" and so on, with a slap on the strings for every "x."

Fills in the verse are full of *slides* (see the Guitar Notation Legend) and *dyads* (see "Brown Eyed Girl"). On the first, use your ring finger to barre the A and D strings while you *slide*. For the second, fret with a pair of fingers, two strings apart, and mute the string in the middle by touching it with the edge of one of those fingers.

Cajun chicken pickin'

The solo is more of the same, in the influential style of Memphis R&B guitarist Steve Cropper. Most of it can be played with a first-finger barre on fret 7 and *hammered* (see the Guitar Notation Legend) notes above. A common way to play the single-note section of the solo is with a kind of "chicken-pickin'" technique, where you mute during the downbeat rests with a downstroke and play the note on the upstroke. This means that you pick up your fretting finger off the frets (but not off the strings) while you pick down, and fret the note when you pick up. You get a "chick-a" effect, hence the poultry reference. To our knowledge, no chickens were harmed in the making of this song!

Rebel, Rebel (page 126)

The ultimate rock chameleon, singer/songwriter and pop icon David Bowie, turned canine for the 1974 album *Diamond Dogs*. The single "Rebel, Rebel" was a song held over from his *Ziggy Stardust* glam phase, and it was later covered by everyone from the Bay City Rollers to the Smashing Pumpkins. Bowie himself played all the guitars on the original.

The pickup

"Rebel, Rebel" starts with a partial *pickup measure*, and the first notes start on "beat 4½." Count, "one–and–two–and–three–and–four–*and*," and start playing on the *and* of beat 4.

The riff

The main guitar part is played around a D–A–E chord pattern. Play the first three notes with your picking hand floating over the strings, so everything rings out; then play the A with a one-finger barre over two strings. After you hit the E chord, quickly *muffle* the strings by laying your right hand over them, and repeat. The next move is a *pull-off* (see the Guitar Notation Legend) and a run down the E chord, one note at a time. After you have this down, you'll never want to stop playing it!

Let ring

At the verse, the instruction "*sim.*" is short for *simile*, as in "similar," as in, "play it the same way you did last time." In other words, let the strings ring out on the first three notes of the riff, and keep it up throughout the song.

The pre-chorus is strummed, with a quick pair of sixteenth notes that anticipates the chord changes on the D and Bm chords. Simply put, strum quickly "down–up–down" with a flick of the wrist, so the chord comes in with a fanfare: "ba-da-bing!" (Pardon the technical term.)

One more note for the end of the chorus: let the E chord ring out, then hit the low E string, third fret (on "beat 3½"), and slowly pull it *downward* for that funky half-step *bend* (see "All Right Now").

Refugee (page 132)

Damn the Torpedoes was the big breakthrough album for Tom Petty & the Heartbreakers. This was one of many hit singles on the album, which pulled the band from bankruptcy to legendary status in 1979. Petty plays rhythm and lead guitarist Mike Campbell adds his signature twang.

The intro, verse, chorus, and solo are based on the same three-chord progression with varying intensity. Start with a full F#m barre chord, then climb up to A5 with the passing note.

Hand shakes

Vibrato is important in Campbell's licks; practice making it a smooth shake of the wrist, not a full-arm spasm. Smooth *bends* are equally important. At intro's end, *bend* the string up a step, then barre the highest two strings with your first finger. Pick them one at a time, then continue with the *slide*, and shake that string!

Play the verse in partial barre chords with a clean tone. The "x's" are just flicks of the pick over *muffled* strings, while your left hand mutes. Kick on the distortion for the pre-chorus, and play the chorus with the same chords and attitude as the intro.

The bridge has some *bends* that need to be precise! They're whole-step *bends*, so each should sound like a note two frets higher than the starting point. Then comes the solo, with *sliding* notes under the open high E string. The middle finger is a good choice for these notes — it's easy to *bend* out of the way of the open string.

Unison bending

In the outro there's more of the same, and the outro solo ends with *unison bends*. Hold the note on fret 14 of the high E string like your life depends on it, and *bend* the B string up (from fret 17) underneath that, repeatedly, then shake it. You should get one thick note that sounds like a chorus of screaming Stratocasters. Visit the Guitar Notation Legend for help with any of the italic terms mentioned here.

Rock and Roll All Nite (page 138)

This song is one of many with "rock" in the title — songs about rock, songs about rockin', and songs about being rocked. Kiss knew how to rock in the wee hours, as evidenced by this classic anthem from *Alive* (1975), originally on their *Dressed to Kill* album (also 1975). With Paul Stanley on rhythm and Ace Frehley on lead, there was much rocking.

Rock tuning

Those of you who grew up with Kiss might know that their tuning of choice is a half step below standard, to compensate for the high-altitude effects on the inner ear caused by wearing platform shoes. You can still play it in standard tuning and standard shoes. (See "Ain't Talkin' 'Bout Love" for more on rock tuning.)

Rockin' triads

Here's the inside scoop on Kiss's preferred method of moving quickly between two major *triads* (three-note chords). Hold a first-finger barre over the D, G, and B strings. Add the middle finger one fret up on the B string, and the ring finger two frets up on the D string. Pick them up; strum. Put them back down; strum. Repeat. This particular move happens in variation all over "Rock and Roll All Nite."

The intro includes the triad move just discussed, played with a stylish *hammer-on* the first time. (Notice the slight change in fingering after you hit the E chord.) Throughout the song, chords are played on "beat 4½," *anticipating* the next measure. Strum with alternating down and upstrokes.

The pre-chorus features a kind of blues rocking (as discussed in "Fun, Fun, Fun"), and the chorus has more of the first technique, same chords.

The solo

Ace's guitar solo is full of blues licks. Start out with a two-string barre on fret 5, under which you *bend* the G string up one step. There's a *two-string bend* that should be pulled downward, and a lick that recurs: a quick *hammer-on* and *pull-off* from fret 5 to 7 and back. Then move up to the top of the neck and repeat the same licks, climaxing with more *bends* and blues-isms. Check out the Guitar Notation Legend for help with any of these terms.

R.O.C.K. in the U.S.A. (A Salute to '60s Rock) (page 143)

In case you forgot how to spell "rock," here's a musical memory booster from the artist formerly known as Cougar. A #2 hit single from the 1985 album *Scarecrow*, "R.O.C.K. in the U.S.A." lives up to its subtitle, both in spirit and in its reference to the pioneers of rock music in the 1960s. Guitarists Larry Crane and Mike Wanchic put the "R.O.C.K." in . . . well, you know.

Getting the feel of the opening chords might be tricky at first. Try playing "up–down" for every open string and chord stab (the opposite of what you might think), then slap your right hand on the strings to mute between strums. When you move up to the Aadd9 and E7, let a finger of your fretting hand touch the D string enough to keep it from ringing out.

Strumming and syncopating

Then comes the strumming — nothing to it, as long as you follow this rule: Your strumming hand should "strum the air" in straight eighth notes when it's not hitting the strings. Notice that some of the verse chords *anticipate* the next beat — the big word used to describe that is *syncopation* or beat displacement. The chorus follows the same pattern with a little variation.

The solo

The guitar solo starts with a *two-string bend*. Use two fingers to push the high E and B strings upward, and let go to play open strings in between bends. When you jump up the neck to play *double stops* (two notes played together on adjacent strings), use one finger over two strings. You can also use one finger to pull the two-string bend on fret 14 downward.

The verse after the solo is played with the intro chord pattern, and the rest of the song is more of the same R.O.C.K.

Rock This Town (page 150)

Here's a swingin' tribute to early rock 'n' roll, complete with towering pompadours and equally big hollowbody guitars and upright basses (plus a tiny little drum kit). Guitarist/vocalist Brian Setzer and the Stray Cats were killer rockabilly revivalists whose 1982 release, *Built for Speed*, made them retro rock stars. Setzer shows his command of the clean tone in "Rock This Town."

Swingin' it

"Rock This Town" rocks with a *shuffle* (or *swing*) *feel*, typical of early rock 'n' roll tunes. Check "The Boys Are Back in Town" for a brief talk on shuffling.

Get ready for some fast strumming, starting with the intro. Play a D chord with a quick "down, up–down–up–down" pattern, then strum more frequently after the band kicks in. Then it breaks down to blues rocking with a *palm mute* (see "Ain't Talkin' 'Bout Love") for the verse. Use *alternate picking* here (up and down picking), so you don't lose the shuffle feel. When Setzer *slides* up to the A chord, he's playing a *partial* barre — first finger over the three highest strings — and filling around that.

The interlude is palm muted again, playing along with the walking bass line. Verse 2 has more fills based around chord shapes, including the song's signature lick: Line your fingers up on frets 12, 11, and 10 in a partial D chord shape, and move the notes around from there.

Shakin' and strummin'

You see lots of fast strumming in the choruses; play those chords in straight, fast down and upstrokes — from the wrist, not the arm. If you have a sore bicep after playing these riffs, you need to correct your strumming technique. Pretend you're shaking water off your hand, and apply that same kind of wrist movement to strumming.

The solos

What can I say about the first guitar solo, except that it's full of *slides*, *double stops* (two notes played together on adjacent strings), *two-string bends*, and *hammer-ons*. Much of the first solo can be played with a partial barre on fret 10. See the Guitar Notation Legend for help with these techniques.

The second solo starts with some *parallel 6ths*, which you play with two separate fingers, two strings apart, muting the string in between by touching it with the edge of a finger. Then you have some bent notes under double stops — hold one finger over the two highest strings on fret 10, and push up the G string from fret 12 underneath.

Rock'n Me (page 160)

Sometimes a song without a guitar solo is refreshing! In "Rock'n Me," Steve Miller tells tales of his job search and transcontinental travels — all for his baby, whom he kindly requests to keep rockin' him. The crafty guitarist/singer/songwriter wove blues, rock, country, and pop into the distinctive sound of the Steve Miller Band, whose 1976 album *Fly Like an Eagle* featured this classic hit.

Keep on riff'n me

The cool main riff starts with two-note *power chords* (see "All Right Now"). Exaggerate the *slide* down from the B5 chord. Play the E5 with a quick down and upstroke. The following lick is played with a first-finger barre on fret 9. Holding the barre, strum down once, *hammer on* fret 11, and strum up once. Repeat five times for a full measure of rock. The third time through the whole riff, jump down to fret 2 for the next lick (with *vibrato* on the top note), then notice the power chords that launch you into the verse. They climb *chromatically* (one fret at a time) from fret 5 to fret 7.

The verse is straight-ahead rock, with a blues-style chord rocking under a *palm mute* (see "Ain't Talkin' 'Bout Love"). Notice how you stay on the same pair of strings throughout the verse and chorus, just moving positions with the chord changes.

The chorus

The chorus has a subtle variation: After "rockin' me baby," let off on the palm mute and stretch the pinky to fret 12, while holding the first finger on fret 7. Repeat the same move on the rest of the chorus chords. And that's everything you need for this nice, compact blues tune. Consult the Guitar Notation Legend for help with terms.

Rocky Mountain Way (page 166)

It's not a song about "rock" per se, though it certainly rocks, in a bluesy kind of way. "Smokin'" Joe Walsh's second solo album, *The Smoker You Drink, the Player You Get* (1973), established Walsh as an inventive rocker whose dry sense of humor and party-animal reputation often made their way into his songs, along with a modicum of smokin' guitar licks.

Slow shufflin'

"Rocky Mountain Way" is played with a slow, ultra-bluesy *shuffle feel*. Think of a slow heartbeat. (Consult "The Boys Are Back in Town" for more shuffling advice.)

The pickup

The intro starts with a partial *pickup* measure. Count off "1, and 2, and 3, *and*" — the guitar starts on the *and* of beat 3.

In between chord stabs on the E5, play the open E string with a *palm mute* (see "Ain't Talkin' 'Bout Love"). Launch into the verse with the ultimate blues lick, pulling the third-fret note slightly after you pick it for a half-step *bend* (see "All Right Now"). Repeat through the verse.

Blues theory?

The bridge has the same bluesy rocking discussed in "Fun, Fun, Fun," which involves moving between the *5th* and *6th* — two different scale tones. That's why you see a different chord symbol above the staff for every note in the bridge.

Everything is straight ahead until the guitar solo, which involves some clever use of *slides*, *staccato* notes, *vibrato*, bends, and of course, *hammer-ons* and *pull-offs*, which are mandatory in rock solos.

Just feel it!

You can look up all the techniques from the solo in the Guitar Notation Legend, but I can't provide a legend that tells you how to *feel* the notes. You can easily forget to pay attention to the feel when reading songs on a page, and in this one, you really don't want to. In this solo, reach for a slovenly, laid-back feeling found somewhere in the reference catalog of your soul.

That weird effect you're hearing in the solo is a talk box; it's a special guitar effect unit with a tube that goes in your mouth! The sound of the guitar essentially replaces your voice box while you manipulate the guitar tone by mouthing words, or "talking."

Shattered *(page 172)*

The Rolling Stones' 1978 album, *Some Girls*, re-established them as a thriving rock 'n' roll institution in the age of disco and punk rock. Elements of both crept into their signature sound in "Shattered." Ron Wood (in his first appearance as a full member of the band) and Keith Richards give you their best attitude riffs in this *power-chord* extravaganza.

Palm power

This tune is built on simple two-note *power chords* (see "All Right Now"), but they're played in all sorts of variations. Play the first E5 chord with a *palm mute*, in a pattern similar to the "Summer of '69" intro. For the following B5, hold fret 4 on the D string while you *hammer-on* from open to fret 2 on the A string. The two chords repeat in variation, and the measure just before the chorus is picked in single notes while you hold the chord down.

The chorus has more chord movement, all power chords with an occasional *slide*.

Ron's riffs

The guitar solo is interesting in that it changes with the chords instead of staying in one scale position — in layman's terms, that means you have to move around the neck a little. Look at the chords first, and try to learn the chord positions that the licks are based on. Key techniques are *double stops* (two notes played together on adjacent strings), *pull-offs*, *bends*, *vibrato*, and more *slides*. The first A5 part is a held barre chord with a *pull-off* on top, and the D5 has *slides* of *parallel 6ths* (see "Rock This Town") with a muted string between. The same occurs over the C5, following an *arpeggio* (a chord played one note at a time). Notice the *pre-bend* on the second E5, played by pushing the string up to pitch before you pick it. Consult the Guitar Notation Legend for help with terms.

The rest of the song is more of what you practiced in the verse and chorus patterns. Notice the ending, a slide from fret 2 to 11, which happens to be the *major 3rd* (scale tone) of E — a perfect note to signal the ending "bonk" on the open E string.

Smoke on the Water *(page 179)*

This song contains the ultimate guitar-store riff, known to those who've never even heard the original. Deep Purple, who had experimented with classically-based and progressive music, became one of the world's most famous hard rock bands — especially after their sixth album, *Machine Head* (1972), which spawned this hit. Deep Purple guitarist Ritchie Blackmore shows you how it's really played!

The immortal opening riff

You can play this with a pick, but know that Blackmore plucked with his fingers on the original. All you need is two strings and a couple fretting fingers to barre the *double stops* (two notes played together on adjacent strings) that make up this mythical riff. Be sure to stop the strings with your right hand wherever there's a rest or a *staccato* dot.

The verse is played in *arpeggios* (chords played one note at a time) with *palm muting* and more *staccato* notes. The chords are simple, but they should be played crisp and clean. The chorus is made of *power chords* (see "All Right Now"), then another rock riff that should be played with barres.

The solo

Ritchie Blackmore's one-of-a-kind soloing style is full of precise *bends*, *pre-bends*, *staccato* playing, fast *vibrato*, neo-classical scale playing, and of course, the mandatory *hammer-ons* and *pull-offs*. You also get to do a lot of *bending* below double stops — hold one finger over the B and E strings while you *bend* the G string up, then play the barred strings. Notice the *bending* lick toward the end of the solo, where you see some strange flat and double-flat signs in front of the notes; that's a *bent* note that you pick while slowly releasing, to get the feeling of a music box slowly running down.

Whammy bar alert

See the big V shape in the tablature with "-2 1/2" at the bottom? That's a *dip* to be played with a vibrato bar, as found on a Stratocaster (or almost any guitar built in the '80s). If you don't have one, you can compensate by bending the guitar neck *slightly* — pushing the back of it with the fretting hand while you push the guitar body inward. But do not push hard or you'll warp (or break) your neck and turn your cherished guitar into instant firewood! Check the Guitar Notation Legend for help with the many techniques in this song.

Summer of '69 (page 185)

Canadian artist Bryan Adams wrote and sang some of the pop anthems of the '80s generation, including this solid mega-hit — ironically, a song about an earlier time. A Top 10 single from the 1984 album *Reckless*, "Summer of '69" captures the spirit of reckless teenagers of all generations. Bryan and lead guitarist Keith Scott wield their Stratocasters with tasteful energy.

Palm reading

If you need some work on *palm muting*, this intro and verse is the perfect exercise. Hold a D chord and strum with all downstrokes, hitting the first and third strokes without muting. For the rest, push down on the strings at the guitar's bridge with the edge of your right hand to get an extra chunky sound.

Economy picking

The pre-chorus is straight strumming, in a "down, down–up, up–down–up" pattern. Then comes the interlude; hold a D chord, but pick up your second finger to start, then pick one note at a time, putting down fingers as the tab dictates. A handy way to pick this is with a kind of economy-picking pattern: "up–up–down–up–up–down," and so on, so that you're sweeping the strings one after another. Use three fingers when you move to the A chord, so that you can move all those notes around while picking.

Notice the added G chord in the second verse. The bridge changes keys (moves to a new tonal center) as shown by the new *key signature*, but the chords are standard. The interlude pattern plays over the chorus, last verse, and outro, so you've got plenty of chances to practice your picking technique!

Sunshine of Your Love (page 193)

The psychedelic blues-rock power trio is a rare species, and Cream was the most famous of them. The timeless guitar/bass riff of "Sunshine of Your Love" will always be part of the rock guitar curriculum, and Eric Clapton's acclaimed guitar solo still gets people squishing up their faces and bouncing their heads in a blues-induced trance. The song was a #5 hit from the 1967 album, *Disraeli Gears*.

Godlike riffing

To play the opening riff, put your ring finger at fret 12, and index at fret 10. Play in that position until you get to the low E string, fret 10. There, you need to shift positions so that your index finger is at fret 8. When you start playing full chords, make them *staccato* (short); lift your fretting hand off the frets (but not off the strings) after each chord to stop the strings.

For the chorus, hit the A chord strumming "down, up–down." After the C chord, hit the muted strings once for a percussive "chick" sound. Likewise with the G chord. End the chorus strumming "down, up–down, up–down," and so on.

Clapton's blues-isms

The guitar solo isn't full of notes and fast playing, but your challenge is to capture the bluesy feel with *bends*, *vibrato*, *slides*, and the obligatory *hammer-ons* and *pull-offs*. Clapton shifts between a couple of different blues-box positions, anchoring the first finger at fret 10 or 7 depending on the lick — sometimes sliding up to fret 13. Where you see two strings *bent* together, pull them downward with one finger. There's also a *two-step bend*, which you should gradually push up to pitch. Check out the Guitar Notation Legend for more on these techniques.

When soloing over the chorus pattern, play mostly off the tenth fret, but whenever you encounter a slide to fret 14, shift up accordingly. One of the licks involves pushing the G string up from fret 12, holding it there, barring the high E and B strings on fret 10, and after playing them, releasing the bend — a classic blues-ism, translated by Clapton and repeated by countless others.

Sweet Home Alabama (page 198)

Open up the encyclopedia of Southern rock, and you'll hear this song playing. (Close it, and you'll still hear this song playing, because the catchy guitar part will never leave your head.) Lynyrd Skynyrd's second album, aptly titled *Second Helping*, featured this 1974 Top 10 hit. With the triple-guitar attack of Allen Collins, Gary Rossington, and Ed King, "Sweet Home Alabama" embodies all that is Southern rock.

Southern fried chicken

Ready for some pickin'? (Grinnin' is optional.) Put your hand in a D chord position, but without the highest note. Pick the opening notes "down, down, up–up–up," then lift up your first finger and put down the middle finger on fret 3. What follows is shown as a quick *palm mute*, but you can also do it with so-called "chicken pickin'." Pick "down–up–down," and on the upstroke, lift your finger off the fret (but not off the string) and put it back down. You should get a "chick-a-chick" sound reminiscent of poultry.

The following licks are played with *hammer-ons*, *pull-offs*, and a whole-step *bend* that's best pulled downward. The verse is a strummed variation of the intro, then comes the interlude. Notice that you start in one position with your index finger barring at fret 7, shift down two frets, then shift down to open position.

Move up to fret 5 for the chorus, and play blues-style with your pinky extending to fret 9. Do the same move at fret 3. On the G chord, strum "down, down, down–up–down," then play the intro riff variation. The second time through, hit an open D string, *hammer on* at fret 2, then quickly play the open G string with an upstroke. Repeat. Repeat again. And again . . .

The solos

The solos are for those with some riffing experience and/or Southern spirit. If you know your scale names, think of them in G major *pentatonic* with a few passing notes. Everything else you need to know is in the tab and the Guitar Notation Legend. Now get in there and give 'em hell!

Takin' Care of Business (page 207)

Question: Is "Takin' Care of Business" a working person's rock anthem, or a sarcastic slam from a musician who doesn't have to work for a living?
Answer: Yes and yes! And in both cases, it rocks.

Bachman-Turner Overdrive II, the second album from the Canadian supergroup, launched this massive hit in 1974. Randy Bachman and his brother Tim take care of the guitar business.

Power-chord thumpin'

The main "TCOB" pattern for the verse and chorus is based on two-note *power chords* (see "All Right Now"). Start with your first and third fingers on frets 8 and 10 as shown, and just put your pinky on 12 to extend the chord. Repeat the same move in a different position for each chord change. Be sure to lift your left hand off the frets (but not off the strings) to create silence wherever there's a rest in the music.

Notice that the first riff, with a *sliding* 7th chord followed by a *hammer-on* and *vibrato*, gets repeated on different frets for the chord changes. The half-step *bend* on fret 6 should be pulled downward. The whole riff gets repeated in variation for the interlude, followed by some *bending* under held notes; put a finger over the high E and B strings at fret 8, and *bend* the G string, fret 10, upward underneath.

The solos

The first guitar solo starts out innocently enough, until you arrive at some *two-string bending* on fret 7; pull downward with one finger. Then come some more *bends* under held strings, ending up with a *held bend* under a fretted note — naturally, use two separate fingers here: one to *bend*, one to hold.

The bridge is played with straight barre chords. Next comes solo number two, starting with a *pre-bend*. You also see where a note is played at fret 10, then *pre-bent* up a half step, picked, and repeated. *Pre-bends* like this should be as precise as you can get them, which can only be achieved with practice, practice, practice. So you see, being a musician takes a little work after all. Consult the Guitar Notation Legend for details on any of these terms.

Tush (page 215)

Billy Gibbons, celebrated guitarist for the Texan blues-rock power trio ZZ Top, had barely begun to grow his beard when this song came out. Now the band has had more hits than facial hairs. "Tush" is an enduring classic rock radio staple from ZZ's fourth album, *Fandango!* (1975).

Shuffle

It wouldn't be a Texan blues-rock song if it didn't *shuffle*, at least a little bit. The shuffle (or *swing*) *feel* is discussed in the performance notes for "The Boys Are Back in Town."

Start with a *palm mute* (see "Ain't Talkin' 'Bout Love") on the low E string, and keep muting that string but not the chords above. You can lay your picking hand on the bridge so that it covers the low string but not the others. This continues until the C7 chord, which you palm mute fully while stretching your pinky to hit the seventh- and eighth-fret notes. Play this with *alternate picking* ("down–up–down–up"), and do the same on the "Lord, take me downtown" part.

Slide guitar

Mr. Gibbons played both guitar solos with a *slide* — not the slide technique, but the bar device you wear on your finger. You can get one at any music store, made of metal or glass. Put it on whatever finger works best for you. Some slide tips:

- ✔ Lay the slide on the strings but *don't press down*!
- ✔ Play over the fret bars — not between them — as if you're playing *harmonics* (see the Guitar Notation Legend).
- ✔ Try to dampen the strings you're not playing.
- ✔ If the slide is on your middle or ring finger, lay another finger on the strings behind it to keep it from buzzing on the frets.

Walk Don't Run (page 220)

There's no greater delight for guitarists than turning up the reverb and shaking their whammy bars on a great surf-rock instrumental. The Ventures' cover of "Walk Don't Run," originally more of a jazz tune by Johnny Smith, hit #2 in 1960 and crowned them the undisputed kings of twang — they're still the biggest instrumental rock group of all time. Two Seattle masonry workers, Bob Bogle (lead guitar) and Don Wilson (rhythm), laid the foundation for generations of twangers to come.

Fingers that do the walking

The full barre chords in the intro are all in the same fingering, starting with an A on fret 5, and moving on down from there. When you get to the open E chord, play it with the same fingers you used for the barre chords; just let your first finger stick out in the air. Then you're in position to jump back up to the A chord.

Play the main melody as if you're in an imaginary C chord position. In other words, use your first finger for all first-fret notes, second finger for all notes on fret 2, and third finger for fret 3. That makes it easier to play the notes smoothly and hit those occasional *dyads* (see "Brown Eyed Girl"), along with the *hammer-ons* and *pull-offs* that make rock guitar great.

The whammy factor

See the words "w/ bar" wherever there's *vibrato*? If you're lucky enough to have a vibrato bar, just give it a fast shake. It helps to hold the bar loosely in your picking hand while you're playing the melody, so it's easy to push it when necessary.

Save your neck!

There are also *dips*, where you pick the note and give the bar a quick push and release, evoking visions of ocean waves and revving hot rods. Some reckless guitarists who don't have whammy bars choose to push down on the guitar body to bend the neck. Avoid this, or you might give your guitar a serious case of whiplash — and your insurance won't cover the chiropractor bills!

Throughout the next section and its *arpeggios* (chords played one note at a time) and *slides*, the melody rarely ventures beyond fret 5, until the groovy ending: a partial C barre chord at fret 8. Give it a whammy-bar dip and vibrato, and yell, "surf's up!" Consult the Guitar Notation Legend for more help on these techniques.

Walk This Way *(page 223)*

Aerosmith was a relatively unknown Boston band when their third album, *Toys in the Attic* (1975), came out, and songs like "Walk This Way" (a Top 10 single) made them a household name for decades to come. Is it rock 'n' roll, heavy metal, glam rock, or funk? Yes, yes, yes, and yes (the song was even re-made with rappers Run-D.M.C. in 1986). Guitarists Joe Perry and Brad Whitford give you a taste of all of the above.

The riff of legends

Here's the must-know intro riff. Pick the first three notes "down–up–down," one finger at a time, so your middle finger ends up on fret 2. Then just bend that finger back to cover the D string, and pick that note with an upstroke. Repeat, and hit the open E string after the second time. The next measure has a *pull-off* from fret 3 to the open string. This is repeated in variation for the interlude.

Now you know the music-store riff; how about the equally-cool verse? Put your hand in a C5 chord with first finger on fret 8 and ring (or middle) finger barring the A and D strings on fret 10. Hold it there, and while *palm muting* (see "Ain't Talkin' 'Bout Love"), pick the notes as shown. Use the *alternate picking* technique with "down–up–down–up, up–down–up," and so on. Your pinky should reach up to frets 12 and 13.

The chorus has the same chord and the same pinky moves, followed by a funky *minor 6th* chord. Just take the fingers you were using on frets 8 and 10, and move them down three strings. Add *vibrato*, and repeat for the F7 chord.

The solos

The first guitar solo stays in one position of the C *blues scale* (which for you technical types is the *pentatonic* scale with an added flat 5th). Joe Perry relies on precise *bends*, quick *hammer-on/pull-off* licks, and fast *vibrato*, all played fast but tastefully. Keep your first finger rooted at fret 8, and you've got a good start.

The second solo is not so innocent, jumping around the scales and positions. The intro riff returns here and is now answered with *bends* on frets 2 and 4, which later jump up an octave to frets 14 and 16. Then there's endless soloing in E — alternating between a box at fret 12, and open position — until the fadeout. See the Guitar Notation Legend for help with the techniques used in this classic tune.

What I Like About You *(page 230)*

The Romantics were a Detroit band influenced by 1960s British Invasion music, punk rock, and a mix of other styles, all adding up to something called power pop. "What I Like About You" was from their self-titled debut album in 1980. The Romantics' finely-coiffed guitarists are Wally Palmar (rhythm) and Mike Skill (lead).

Three-chord classic

"What I Like About You" is based on a classic three-chord pattern (also heard in "R.O.C.K. in the U.S.A.") and variations of it. For the intro, start with an E barre chord at fret 7, and add other fingers as shown to change chords. Then jump down to open D and A chords, and repeat the whole thing.

Strumming

The verse and chorus are played in a repeated two-measure strum pattern: "down, down–up–down, down–up–down, down–up, up–down–up." Your strumming hand should be bouncing in constant eighth notes, and "missing" the strings whenever there's a break in the strumming. Chord-wise, you're moving up and down the strings at the bottom of the neck.

The guitar "solo" is really just a chord pattern with fills. Strum the first chord quickly, "down–up–down," then bend up the G string at fret 2 while holding the B string at fret 3. After you hit the A5 chord, play a straight A (with one finger barring three strings), then hold that position and put your middle and third fingers on frets 3 and 4, respectively. In the next measure, repeat the same move two frets higher. Be sure to mute the strings wherever you see a rest.

After the B barre chord, you continue playing through the harmonica solo and the rest of the tune, with the same tried-and-true power pop pattern. Repeat the intro riff at the end.

Wild Thing (page 235)

Long before punk rock and power pop were part of the rock vocabulary, bands like the Troggs blasted the way. Their wall of sound was the inspiration for what became known as "garage rock," and record numbers of neighbors have complained about the volume of songs such as "Wild Thing" ever since. The song was a #1 hit in 1966, and guitarist Chris Britton helped build the wall of barre chords.

Begin slightly bent

Is there a cooler way to start a song than with a *pre-bend*? From fret 6, push the G string up a step, then pick it and slowly bring it down. To find your starting pitch, first play an unbent note on fret 8; then you'll know what your pre-bent note should sound like.

Wall of inversions

Play the song in full barre chords; part of what creates that massive sound is including the low E string in all the chords. When you play the D chord, holding that lowest note turns it into a thick kind of *inversion* — a chord with a note other than the root (D) on the bottom. (Inversion is also a big word you can use to impress your jazz-musician friends.)

Strumming

The main strumming pattern has some *muffled* notes — places where you strum with your hand laid over the strings for a percussive "click" sound. The first one is played as a quick upstroke, so the best way to play the pattern is something like "down, down, *rest*, up–down, down, (up)." On *rest*, just plop your picking hand on the strings to keep them from ringing.

Chord changes in the verse are equally groovy: Barre the fifth fret with your index finger, strum, and put down the rest of your fingers to form an A chord. Repeat. Hold your picking hand up high for the audience.

Aside from a pause before the recorder solo and some straight strumming of the E chord, that's it. On a guitar song like this, its grooviness is in its simplicity, man.

Won't Get Fooled Again (page 240)

From the 1971 album *Who's Next*, "Won't Get Fooled Again" is one of those rock anthems that always gets cranked up on car radios. (Drivers should exercise caution when playing air-windmill chords in heavy traffic.) Pete Townshend of the Who alternates *power chords* (see "All Right Now") with blues licks in this epic song.

The ultimate power chord

The opening power chord is a partial version of one that dominates this song: a fully stacked A5 with a double barre. Put your first finger in a barre across the D and G strings on fret 2. Now barre your pinky on fret 5 across the B and high E strings (mute or leave out the low E string). Strum, and feel the power.

Play the lead licks and chords casually throughout this song. You'll note a lot of playing off of that main chord and the open A string, with space in between. When moving to the E5, first hit fret 3 on the E string and pull it *downward* for a half-step *bend*. Then the E is just open strings, and the next chords have certain strings muted for a spacious sound.

The chorus, fool

The chorus moves between the big A chord and D, but not all notes are played at once. The following lick is in a blues box between frets 8 and 10. *Pre-bend* the first note, and pull the next bend downward a quarter step. See more about *bends* in the Guitar Notation Legend.

The bridge has more power chords and fills around them, including another quarter-step bend alternating with a fretted note — pick this "down–up–down–up." Under "get all my papers," play the fill from the position of that main A5 chord, with barres on frets 2 and 5.

For the guitar solo, Townshend jumps between two blues boxes in B major and minor *pentatonic* — but don't sweat the scales, just follow the tab. For the interlude, make sure the strings are muted right away after the G5 and D chords — take pressure off the chords while covering the strings.

The rest of the song is varied around the same chords and licks. Now that you've got the main Townshend-isms down, you can apply them to what you see on the tab, and you won't be fooled again.

You Give Love a Bad Name *(page 248)*

Bon Jovi was one of few bands to emerge from the arena rock/"hair band" scene of the '80s to become an enduring force in pop music — with help from a good barber and strong pop/rock songs. This #1 single from the 1986 album *Slippery When Wet* features the slippery guitar licks of Richie Sambora.

The intro is a lesson on blues licks. *Bend* the G string up a whole step from fret 10, let it down and shake it. When you do a quarter-step *bend*, pull the string downward slightly. The lick over the E♭5 is a *bend*, *release*, and *pull-off*, all in one smooth motion.

Pinch those harmonics!

The next pattern is played with *palm muting* and *pinch harmonics*. Where the sheet music says "P.H." (shorthand for pinch harmonics), turn your pick on its edge, so that the side of your thumb grazes the string and you hear a screeching overtone on top of the main note. (The overtone will change depending on where your picking hand is along the string.)

Dip that bar!

The next lick requires a vibrato bar for the *dips*, and so do the fills in the pre-chorus, including a gradual *dive*, more *dips*, and the kind of *vibrato* that only a bar will give you. The chords under that are played in *arpeggios*, one note at a time.

The chorus is straight *power chords* (see "All Right Now"), all played on the same pair of strings. Then comes the solo with more whammy-bar *diving* and *vibrato*, plus a climbing riff made of *sliding octaves*. Starting with the index finger on fret 3 and ring (or pinky) on fret 5, let the edge of one finger touch the string in between to mute it. From there you can pick across all three strings and *slide* as shown in the tab.

Tap that pick!

The next technique is straight out of the '80s rock school. Play a pair of *hammer-ons* and *pull-offs* as shown, then tap on fret 13 with the pick, and *slide* it up. Practice this lick slowly, and steadily work it up to Sambora speed. The pick-tapping is followed by *unison bends*, a *palm-muted* variation on the verse lick, and of course, a final whammy-bar *dive*. If you're unfamiliar with any of these techniques, consult the Guitar Notation Legend.

Ain't Talkin' 'Bout Love

Words and Music by David Lee Roth, Edward Van Halen, Alex Van Halen and Michael Anthony

Tune down 1/2 step:
(low to high) Eb-Ab-Db-Gb-Bb-Eb

Intro
Moderate Rock ♩ = 138

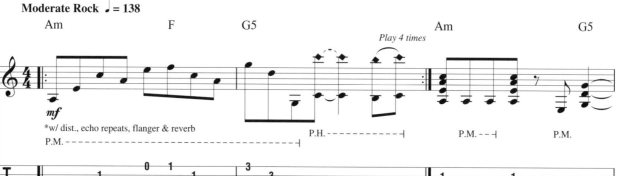

*Set echo at approx. 100ms delay.
Set flanger for slow speed w/ regeneration sweep and moderate depth.

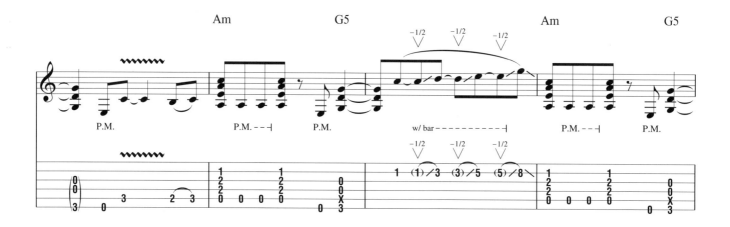

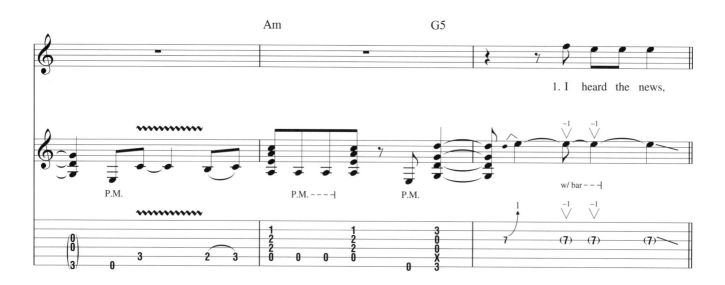

1. I heard the news,

*Hold bend while sliding.

Guitar Solo

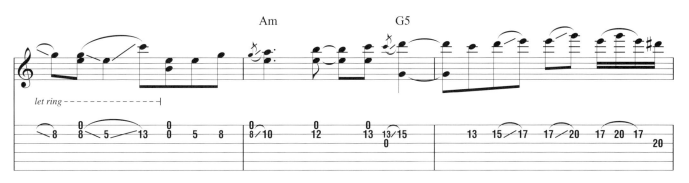

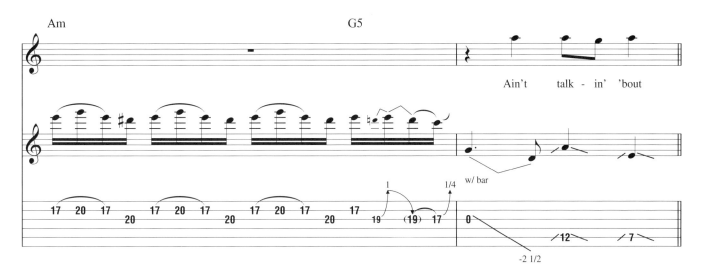

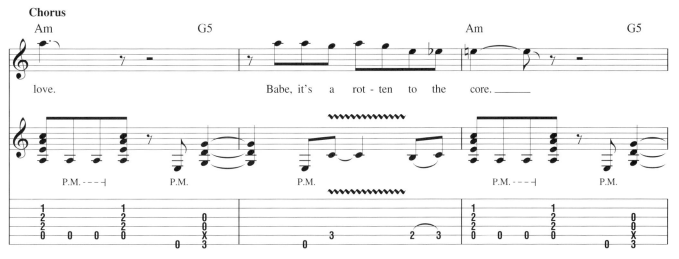

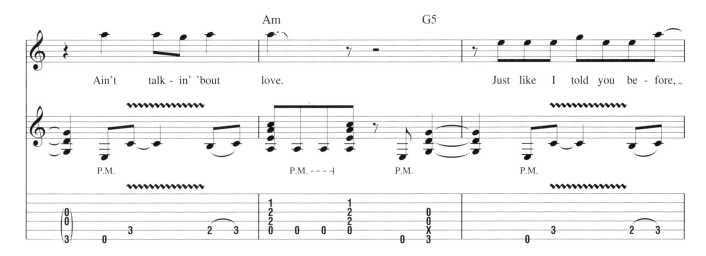

*Lower vol. knob about halfway to produce a slightly distorted tone.

Pitch: D G B

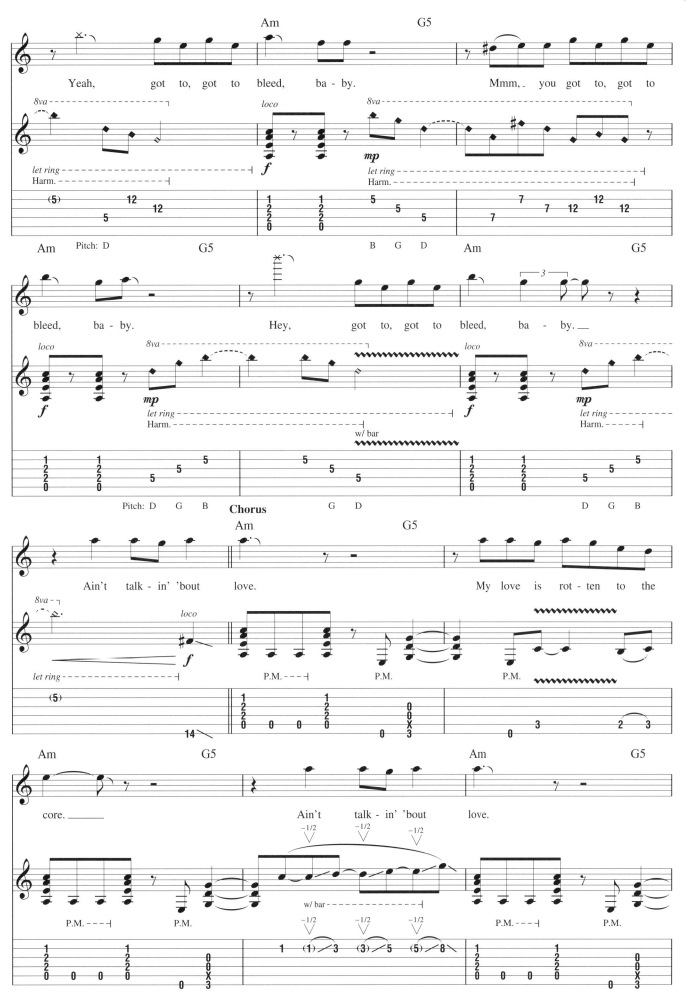

Additional Lyrics

2. You know you're semi good lookin',
   And on the streets again.
   Oh, yeah, you think you're really cookin', baby.
   You better find yourself a friend, my friend.

All Right Now

Words and Music by Paul Rodgers and Andy Fraser

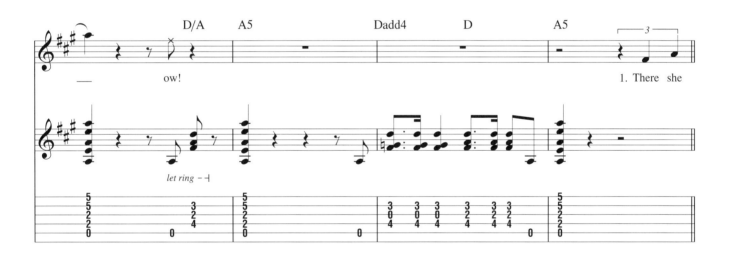

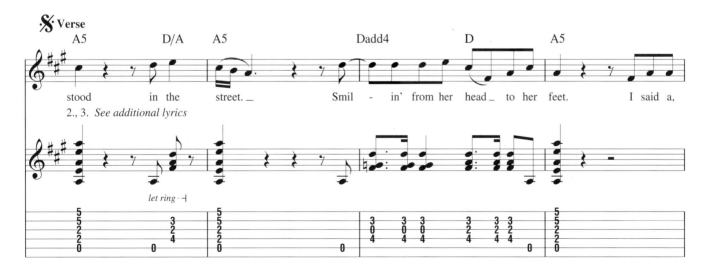

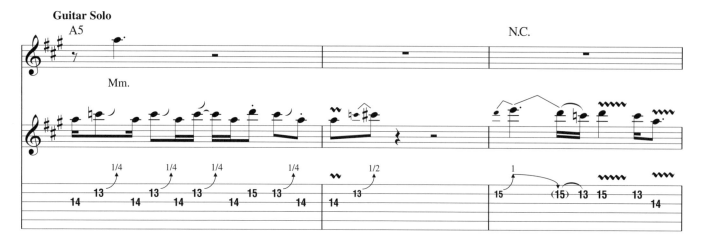

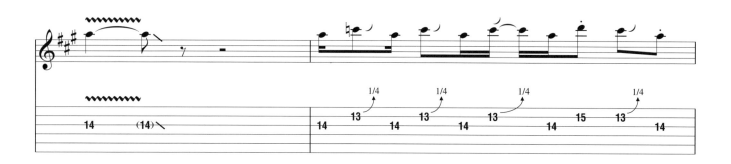

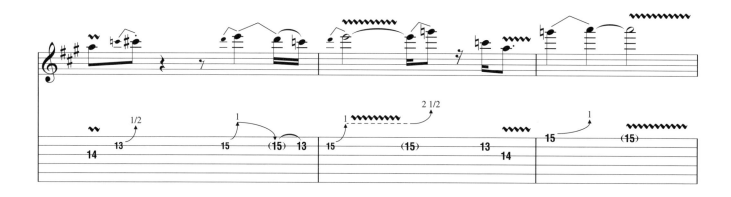

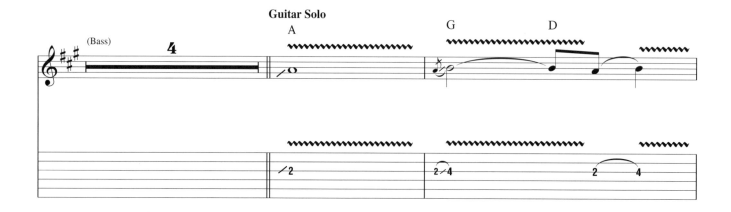

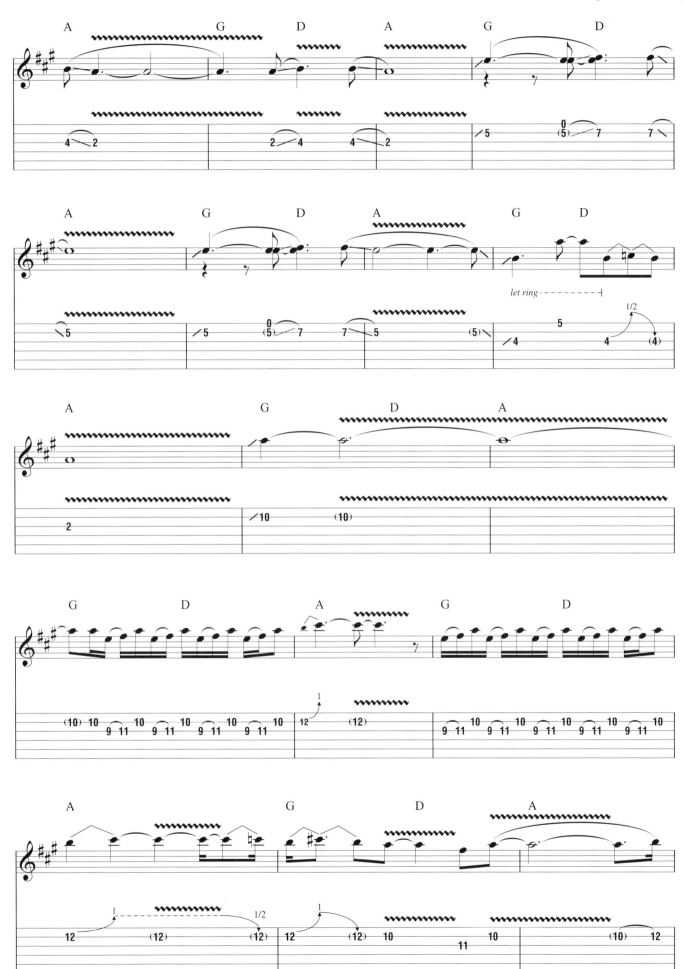

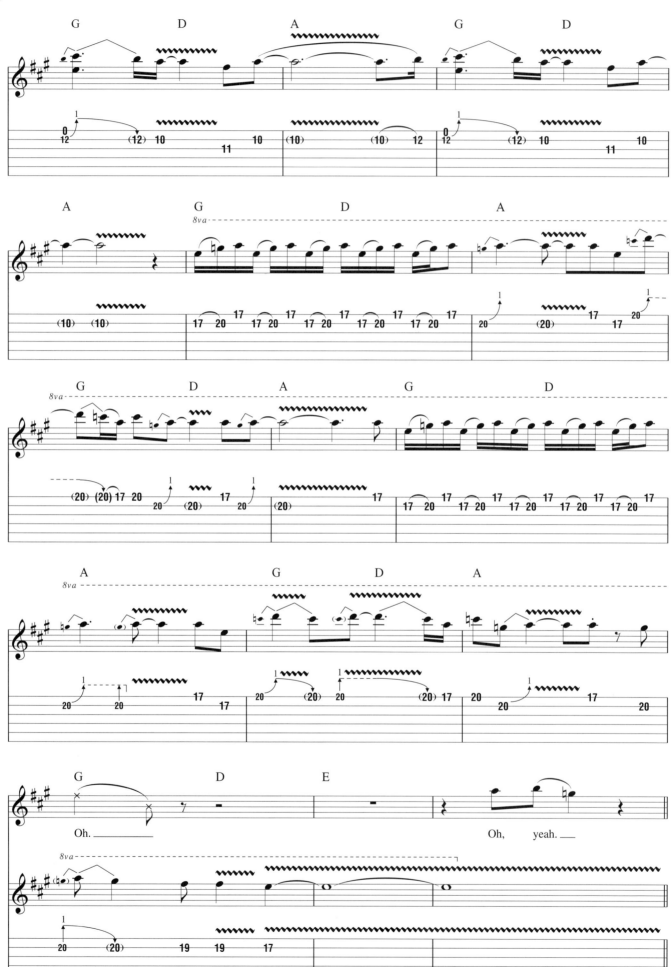

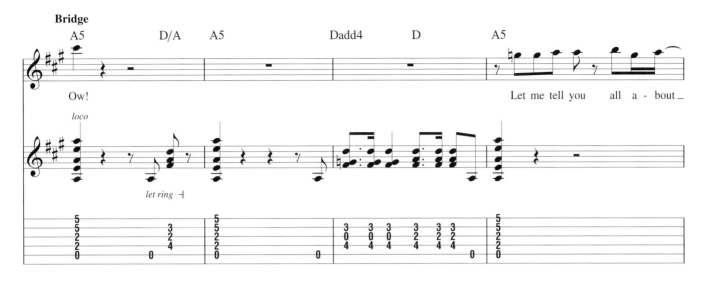

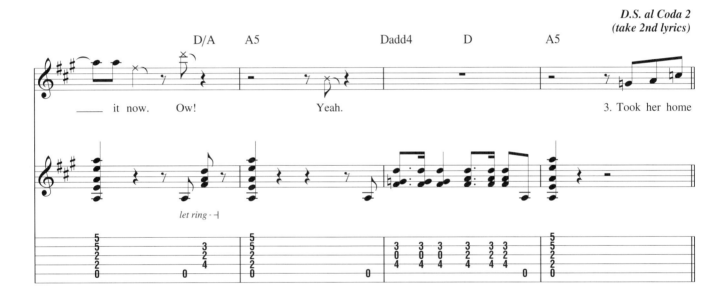

py to-geth-er. Ow! It's all right, it's all right, it's all right.____ Ev-'ry-thing's all right.

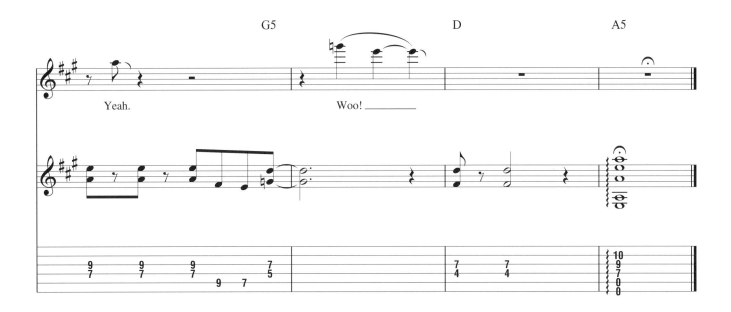

Yeah. Woo!_____

Additional Lyrics

2., 3. I took her home to my place,
Watching ev'ry move on her face.
She said, "Look, what's your game, baby,
Are you tryin' to put me in shame?"
I said, "Slow, don't go so fast,
Don't you think that love can last?"
She said, "Love, Lord above,
Now you're tryin' to trick me in love."

Born to Be Wild

Words and Music by Mars Bonfire

Pre-Chorus

Yeah, dar - lin' go make it hap - pen,

2nd time, substitute Fill 1

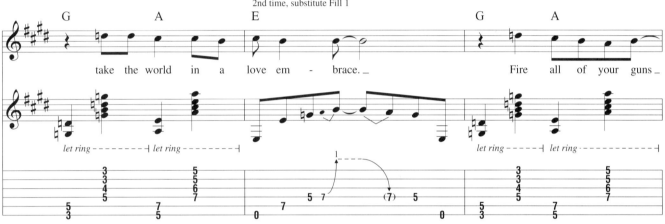

take the world in a love em - brace. Fire all of your guns

2nd time, substitute Fill 2
3rd time, substitute Fill 3

1.

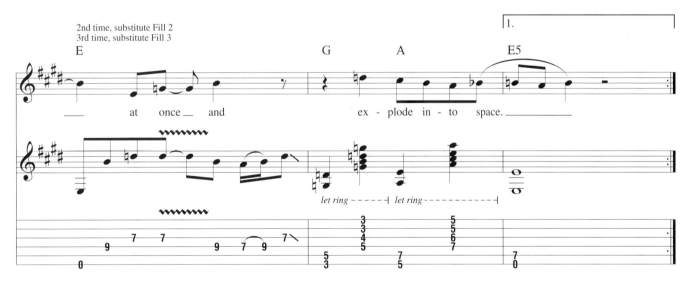

____ at once __ and ex - plode in - to space. _____

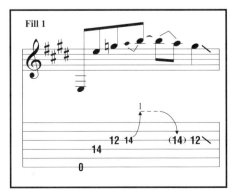

Fill 1

Fill 2

grad.
release

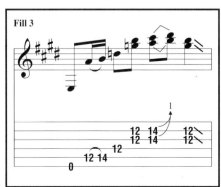

Fill 3

Additional Lyrics

2. I like smoke and lightning,
Heavy metal thunder,
Racin' with the wind,
And the feelin' that I'm under.

The Boys Are Back in Town

Words and Music by Philip Parris Lynott

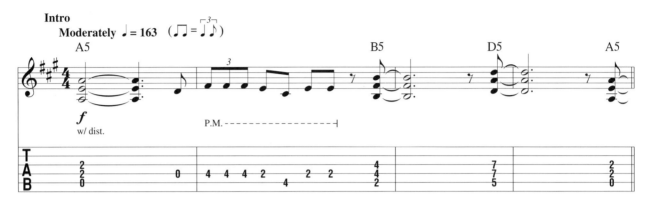

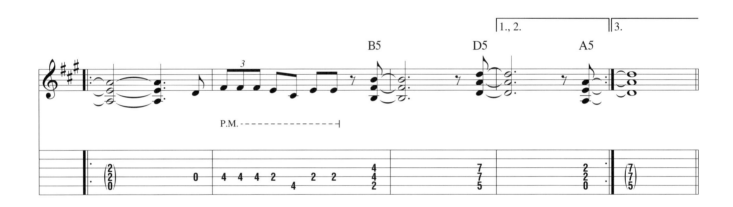

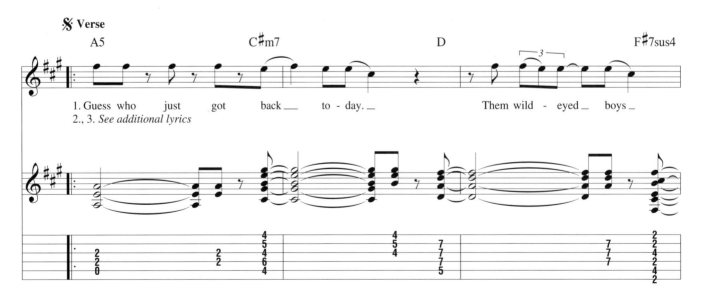

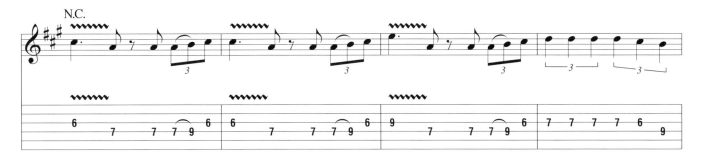

Bridge

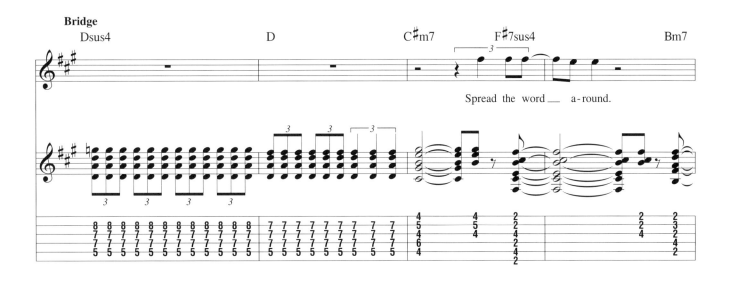

Spread the word ___ a-round.

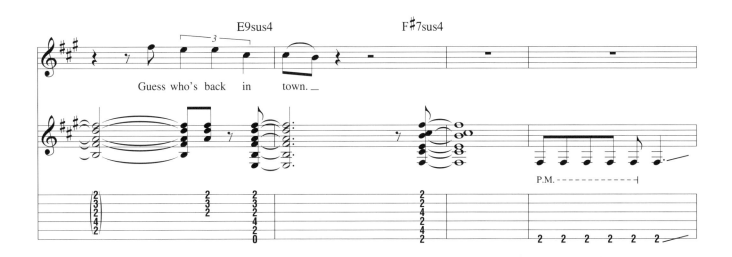

Guess who's back in town. ___

You spread the word a-round.

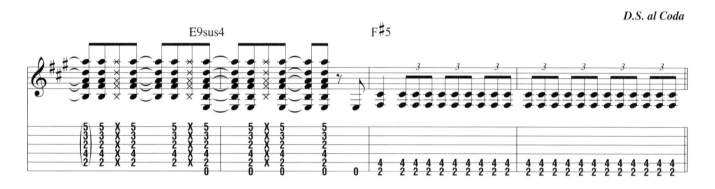

D.S. al Coda

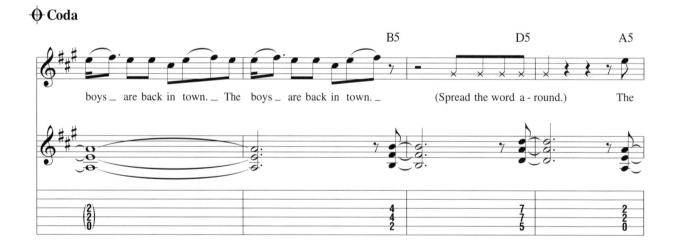

⊕ **Coda**

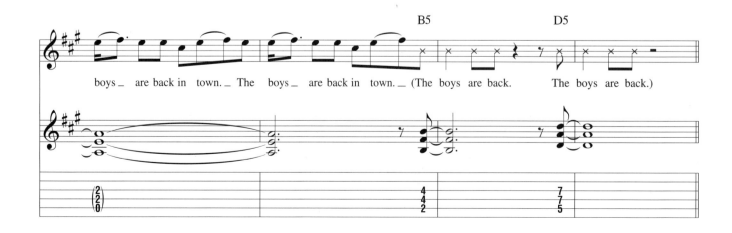

boys are back in town. The boys are back in town. (Spread the word a-round.) The

boys are back in town. The boys are back in town. (The boys are back. The boys are back.)

Interlude

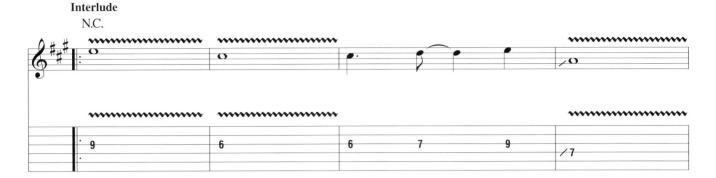

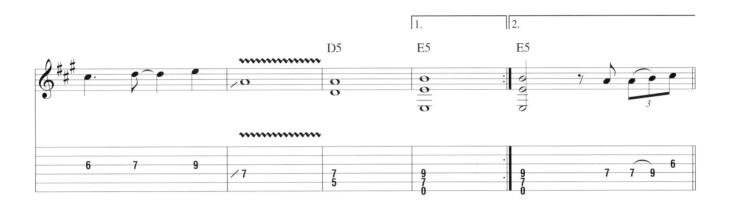

Repeat and fade

Outro

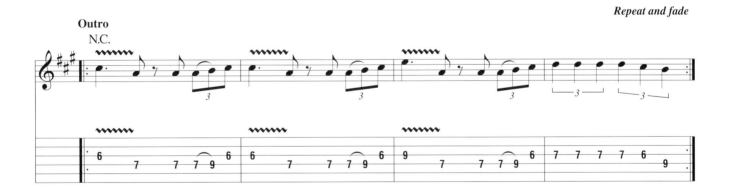

Additional Lyrics

2. You know that chick that used to dance a lot?
   Every night she'd be on the floor shakin' what she got.
   Man, when I tell you she was cool, she was red hot.
   I mean she was steamin'.
   And that time over at Johnny's place,
   Well, this chick got up and she slapped Johnny's face.
   Man, we just fell about the place.
   If that chick don't want to know, forget her.

3. Friday night they'll be dressed to kill
   Down at Dino's Bar and Grill.
   The drink will flow and blood will spill,
   And if the boys wanna fight, you better let 'em.
   That jukebox in the corner blasting out my favorite song.
   The nights are getting warmer, it won't be long.
   Won't be long till summer comes,
   Now that the boys are here again.

Brown Eyed Girl

Words and Music by Van Morrison

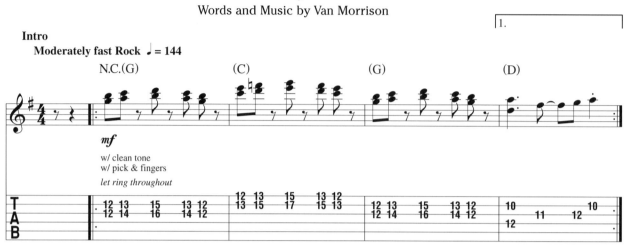

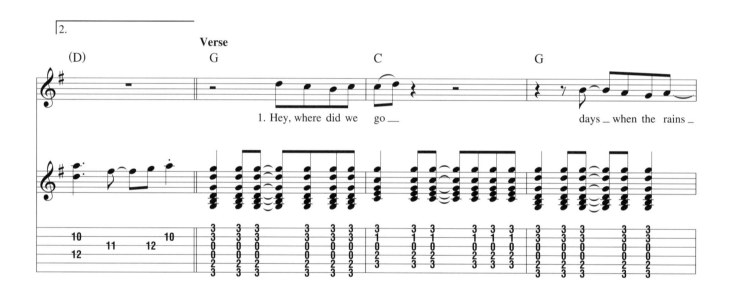

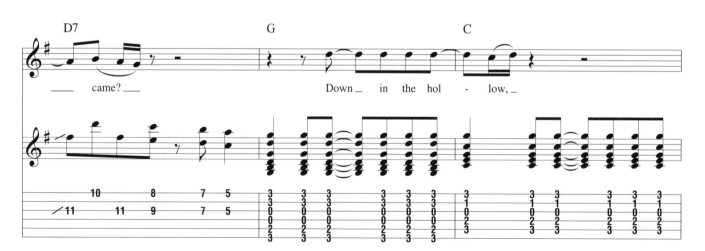

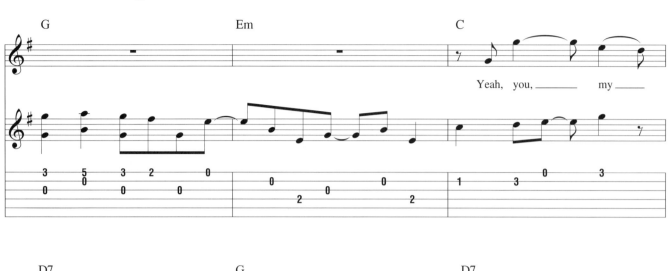

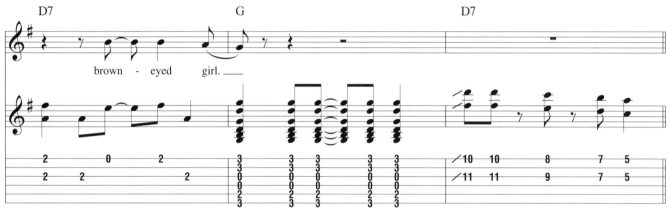

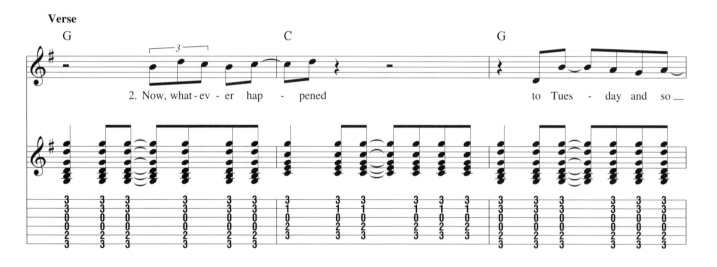

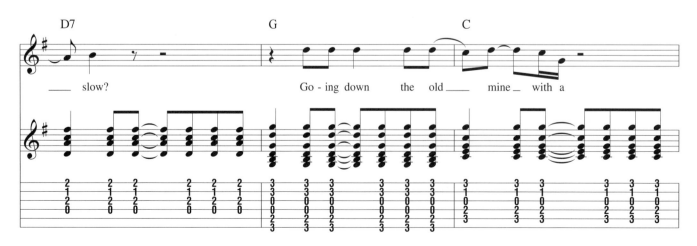

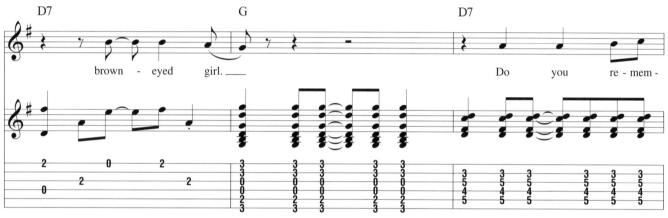

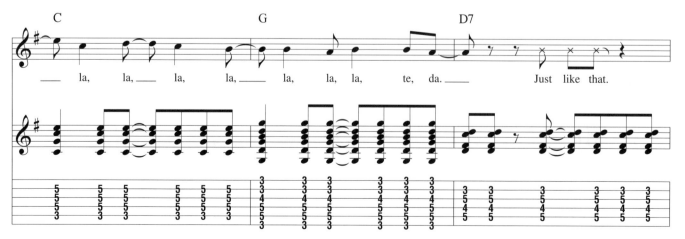

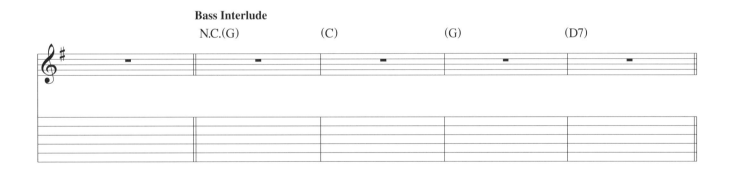

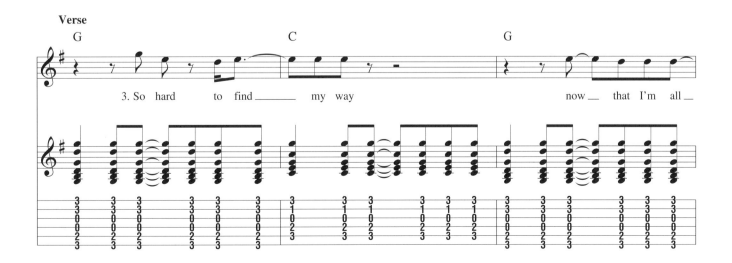

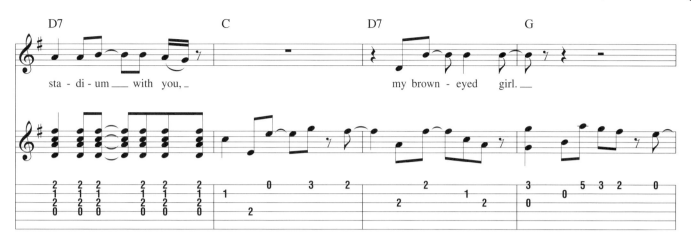

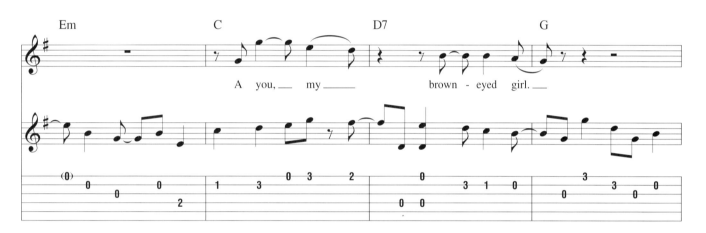

Play 4 times & fade

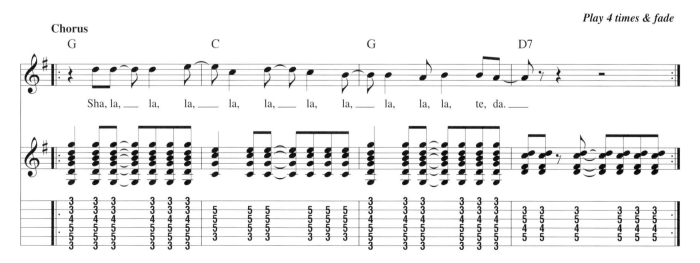

Drive My Car

Words and Music by John Lennon and Paul McCartney

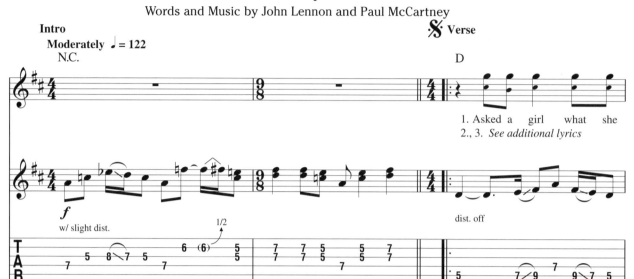

Guitar Solo

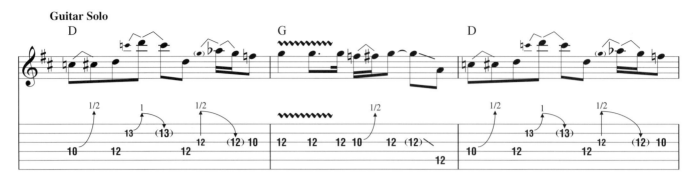

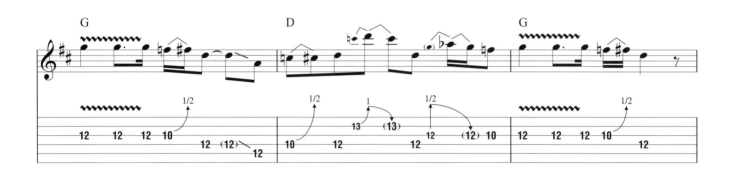

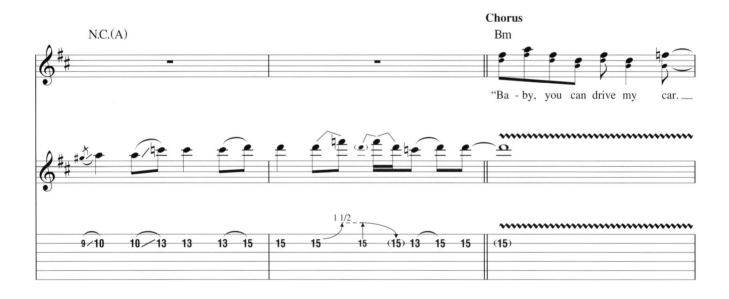

D.S. al Coda

Additional Lyrics

2. I told that girl that my prospects were good,
   She said, "Baby, it's understood.
   Workin' for peanuts is all very fine.
   But I can show you a better time.

3. I told that girl I could start right away,
   And she said, "Listen babe, I got somethin' to say.
   I got no car and it's breakin' my heart,
   But I found a driver and that's a start.

Fun, Fun, Fun

Words and Music by Brian Wilson and Mike Love

Tune down 1/2 step:
(low to high) E♭-A♭-D♭-G♭-B♭-E♭

Intro

Moderately fast ♩ = 168

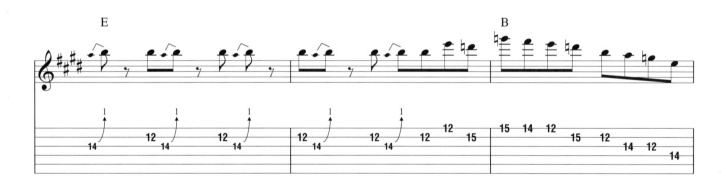

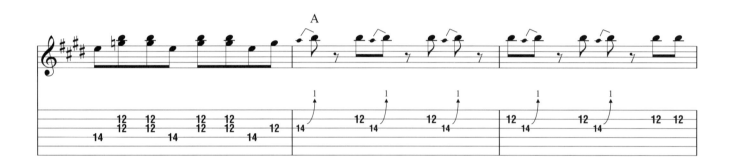

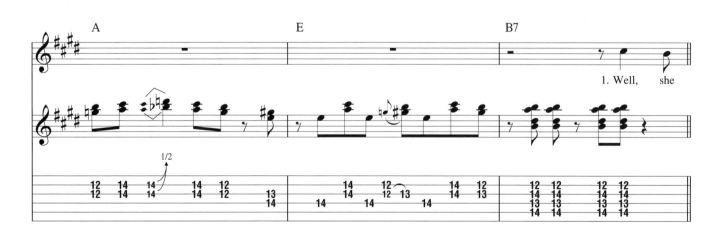

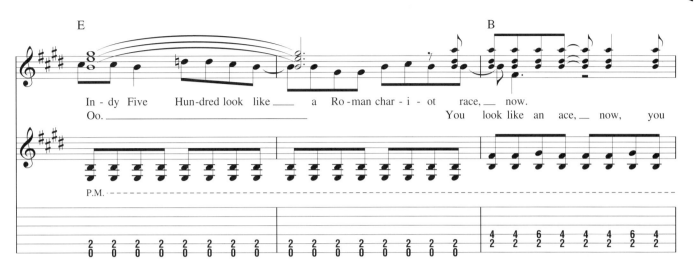

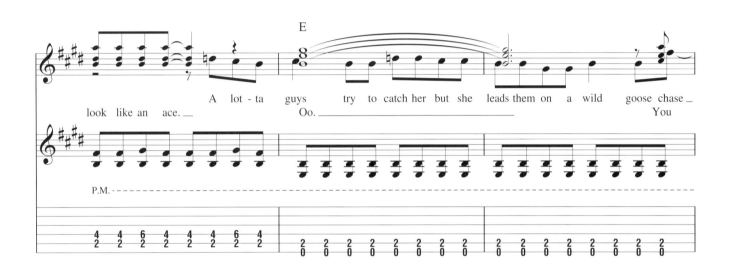

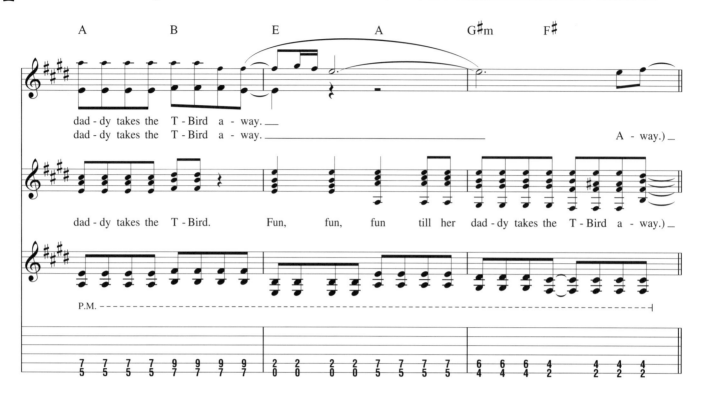

dad - dy takes the T - Bird a - way. ___
dad - dy takes the T - Bird a - way. _____

A - way.) ___

dad - dy takes the T - Bird.   Fun,   fun,   fun   till   her   dad - dy takes the   T - Bird a - way.) ___

P.M. --

Guitar Solo

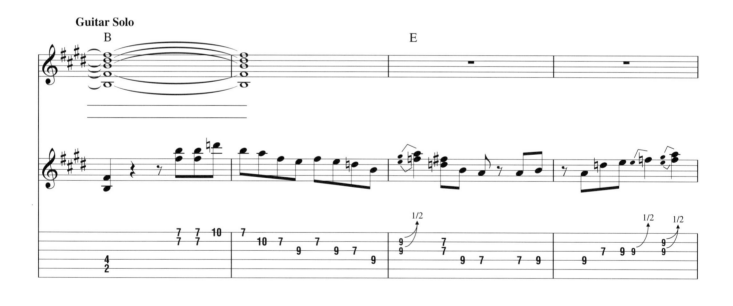

D.S. al Coda

3. Well, you

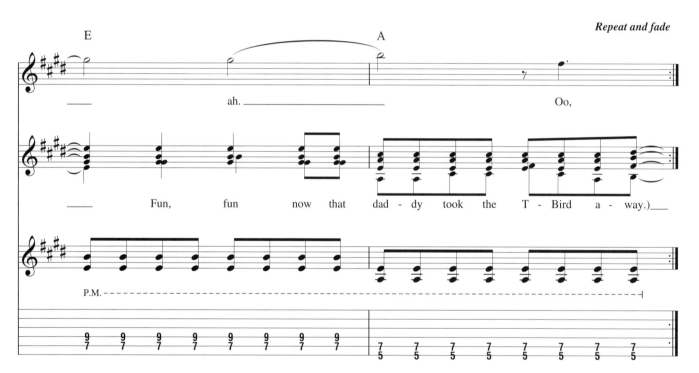

Additional Lyrics

3. Well, you knew all along
   That your dad was gettin' wise to you, now.
   (You shouldn't have lied, now, you shouldn't have lied.)
   And since he took your set of keys
   You've been thinkin' that your fun is all through, now.
   (You shouldn't have lied, now, you shouldn't have lied.)
   But you can come along with me
   'Cause we got a lotta things to do now.
   (You shouldn't have lied, now, you shouldn't have lied.)
   And we'll..

Hey Joe

Words and Music by Billy Roberts

Intro
Moderately slow Rock ♩ = 82

N.C.(E7)

mf
w/ dist.

Verse

C   G   D   A

1. Hey _____ Joe,   uh, where you go - in' with that

*T

T

*T = Thumb on 6th string

E   C   G

gun in your hand?   Hey _____ Joe,

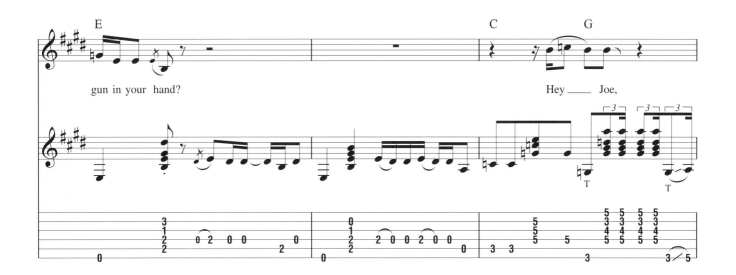

T   T

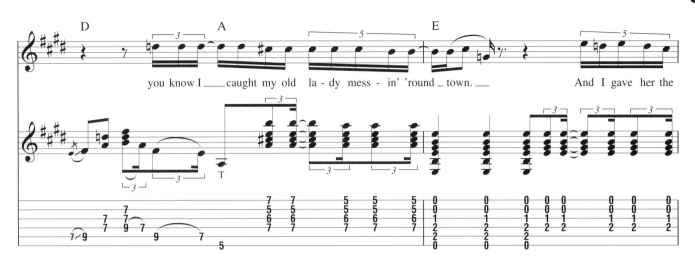

you know I ____ caught my old la - dy mess - in' 'round ____ town. ____ And I gave her the

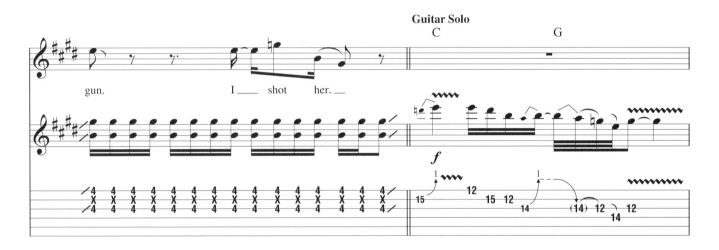

Guitar Solo

gun. I ____ shot her. ____

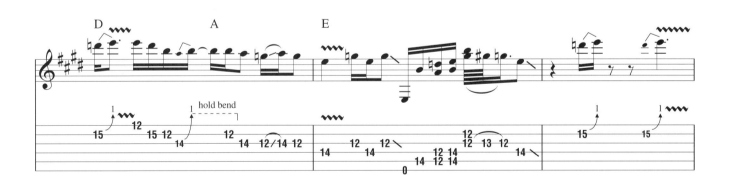

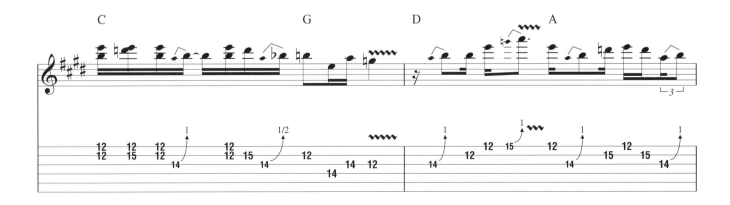

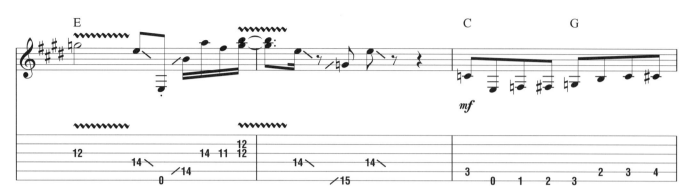

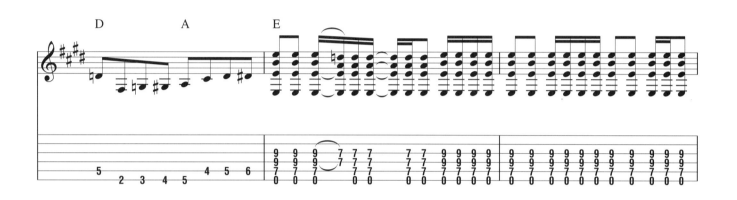

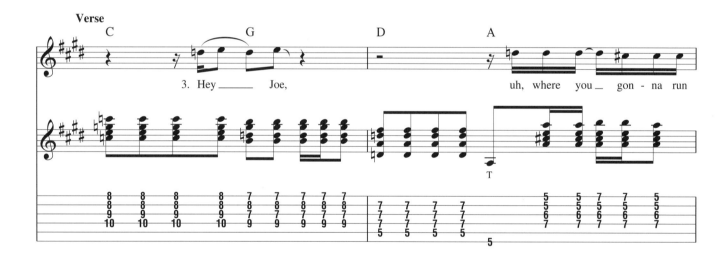

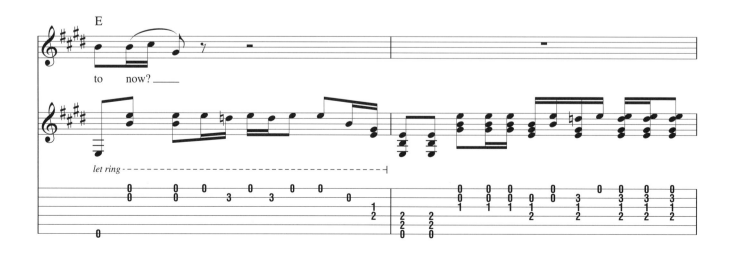

Hit Me With Your Best Shot

Words and Music by Eddie Schwartz

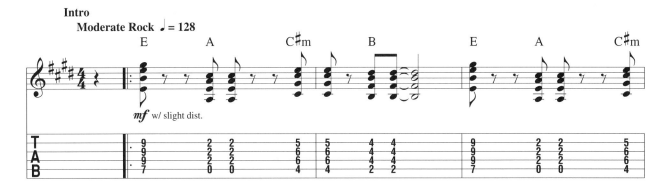

1. Well, you're a real tough cook-ie with a
2. *See additional lyrics*

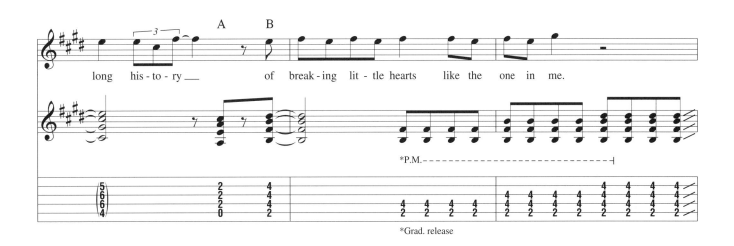

long his-to-ry ___ of break-ing lit-tle hearts like the one in me.

*P.M.

*Grad. release

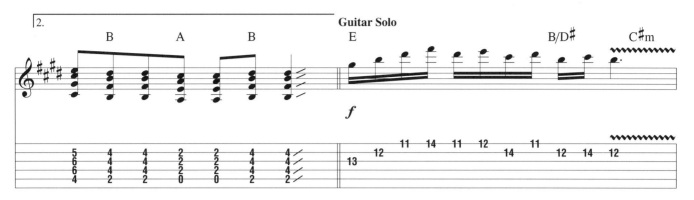

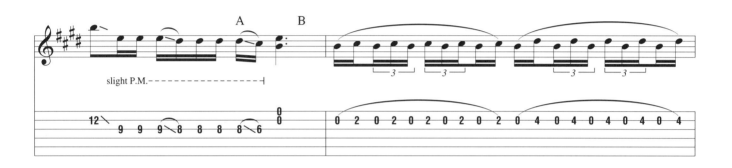

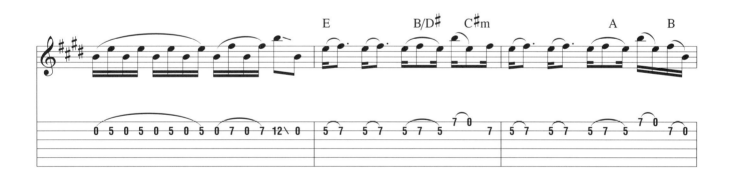

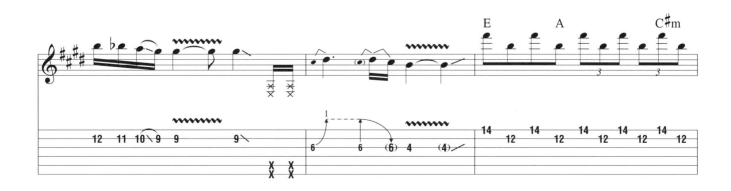

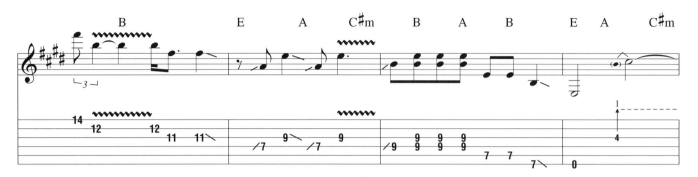

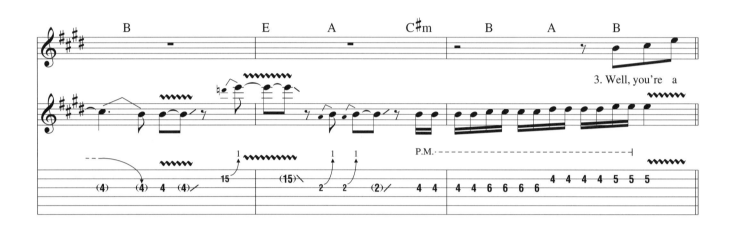

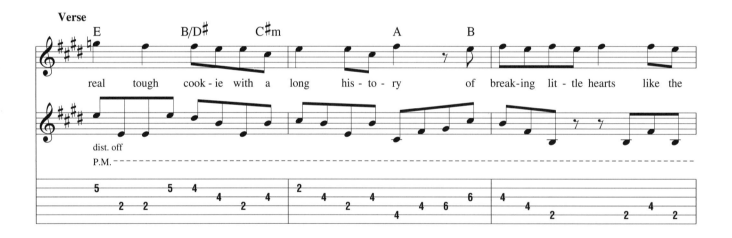

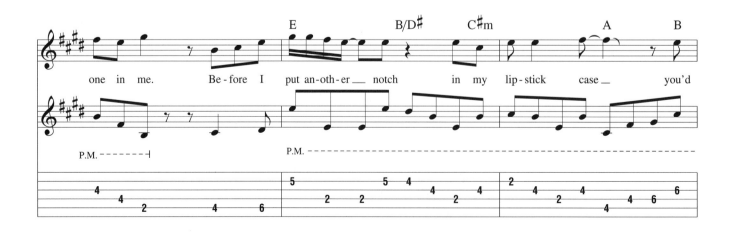

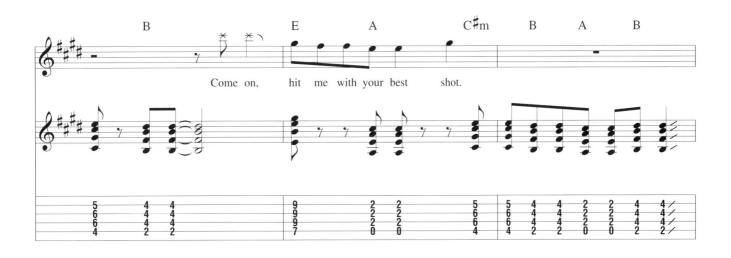

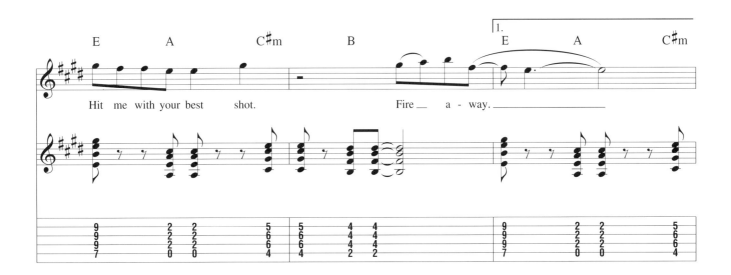

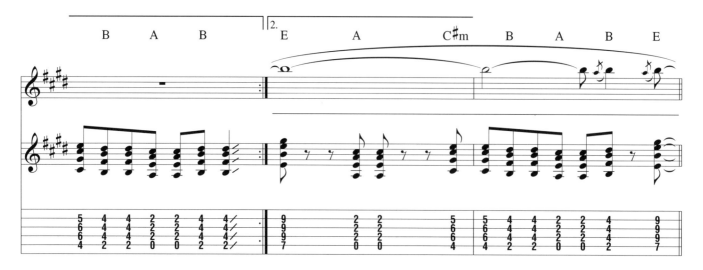

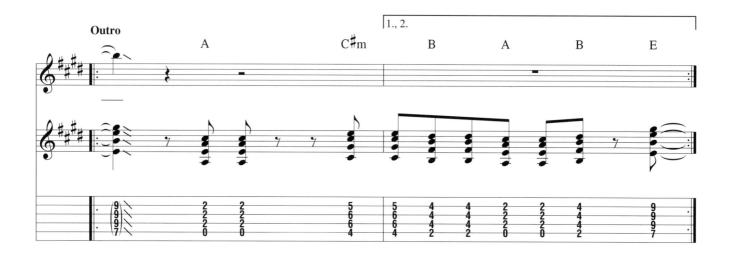

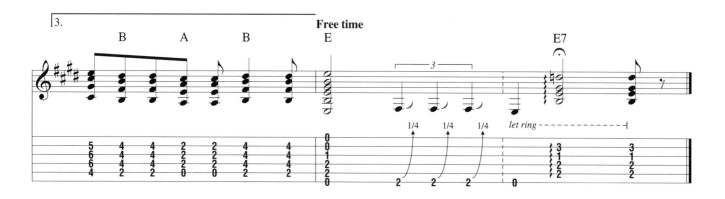

Additional Lyrics

2. You come on with a come on, you don't fight fair.
    But that's okay, see if I care.
    Knock me down, it's all in vain.
    I'll get right back on my feet again.

I Want You to Want Me

Words and Music by Rick Nielsen

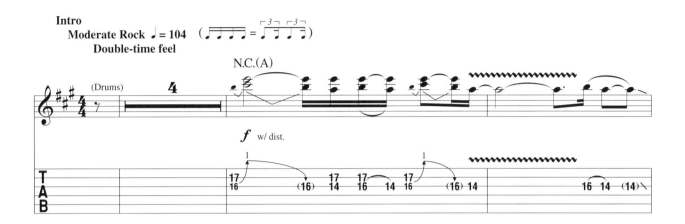

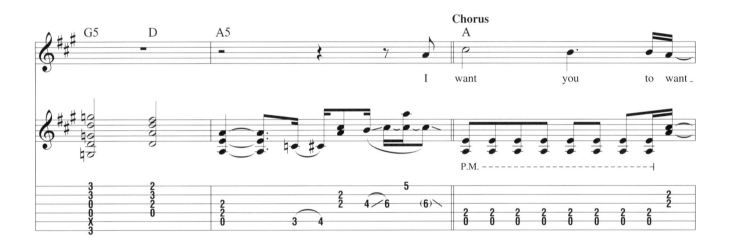

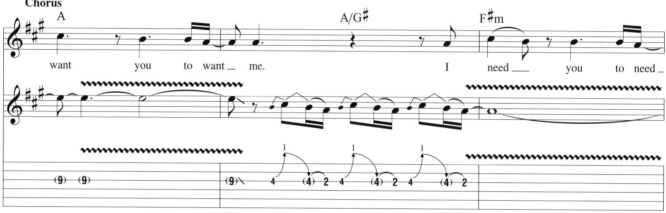

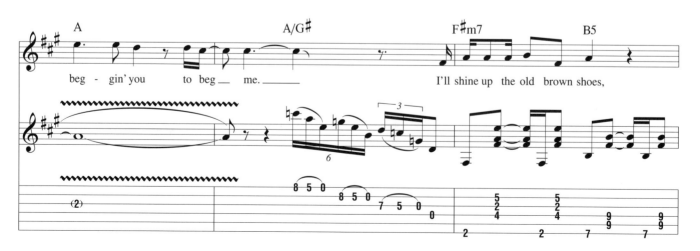

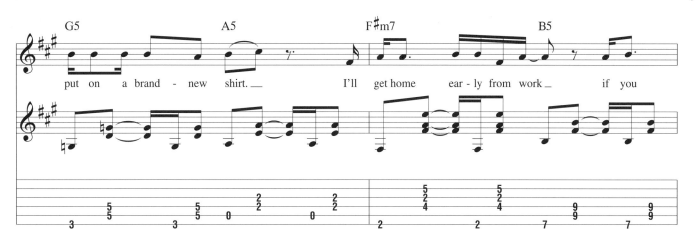

put on a brand - new shirt. ___ I'll get home ear - ly from work ___ if you

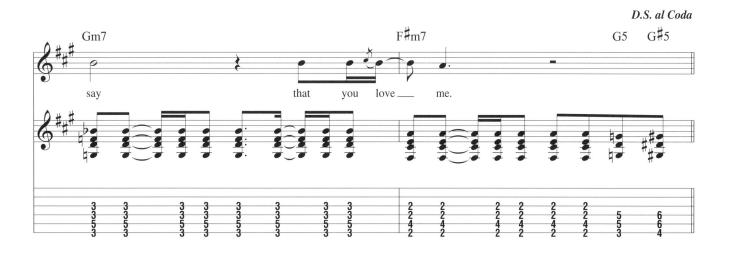

D.S. al Coda

say that you love ___ me.

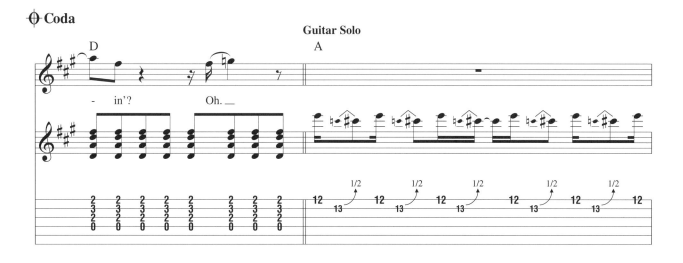

⊕ Coda

Guitar Solo

- in'? Oh. ___

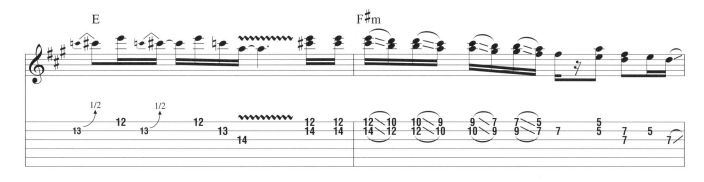

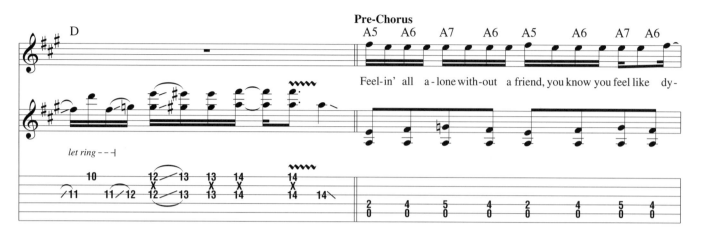

Pre-Chorus

Feel-in' all a-lone with-out a friend, you know you feel like dy-

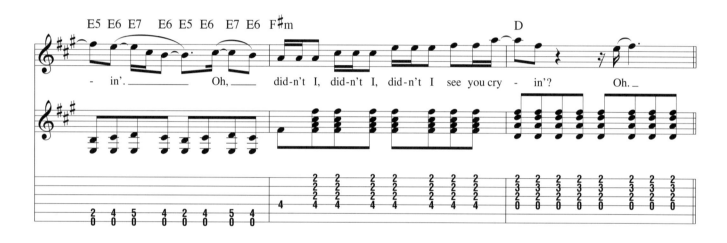

- in'._____ Oh,_____ did-n't I, did-n't I, did-n't I see you cry - in'? Oh. _

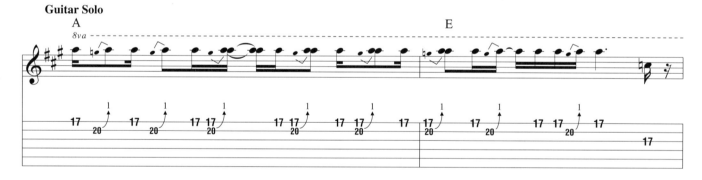

Guitar Solo

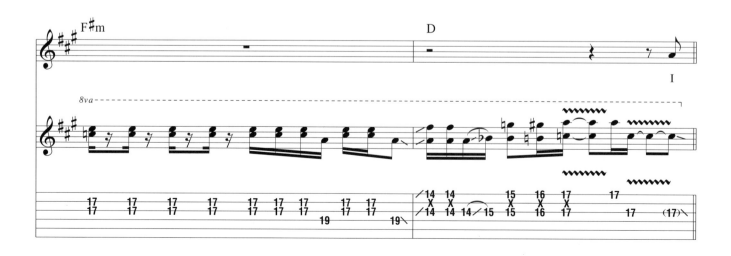

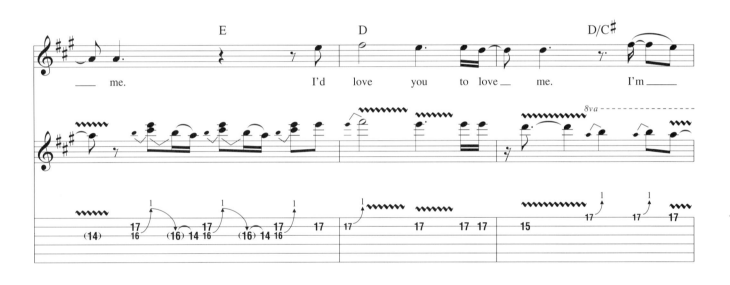

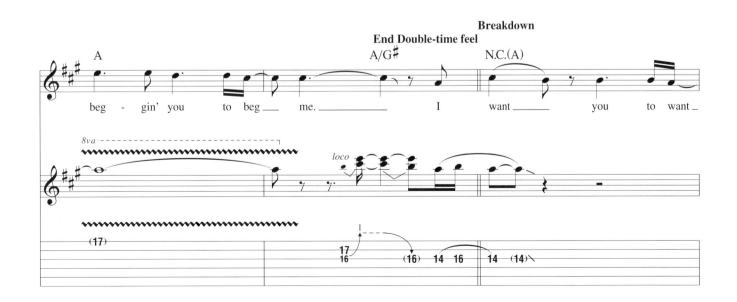

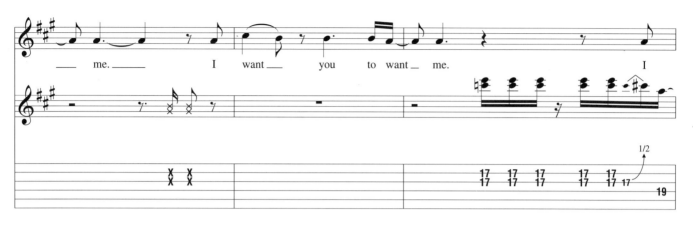

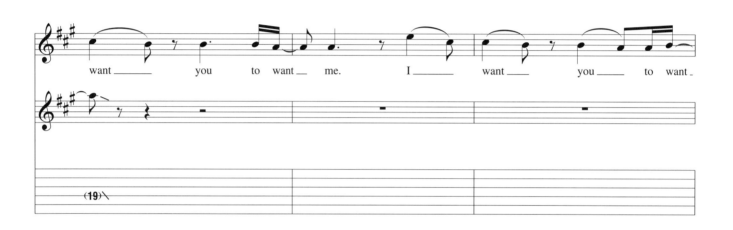

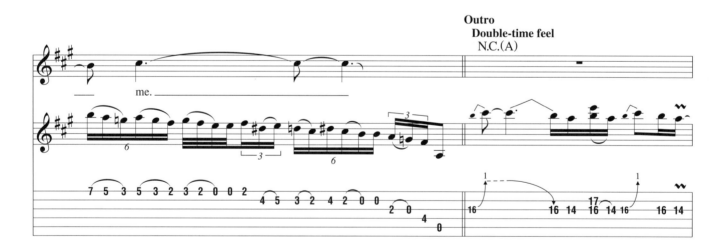

Message in a Bottle

Words and Music by Sting

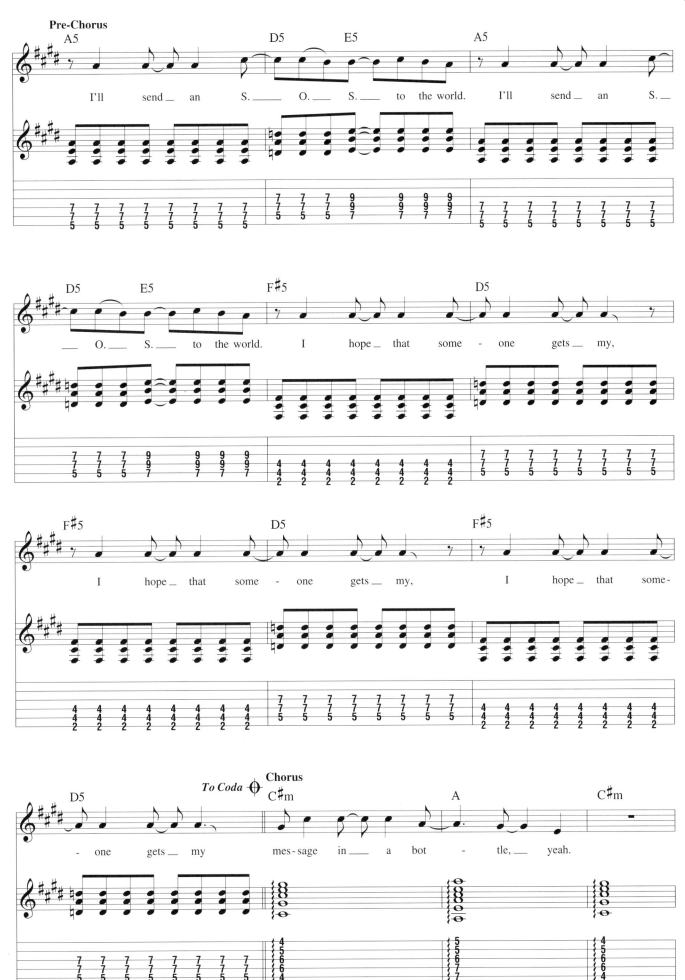

Mes - sage in __ a bot - tle, __ yeah.

Oh. _____

Mes - sage in __ a bot - tle, __ yeah.

D.S. al Coda

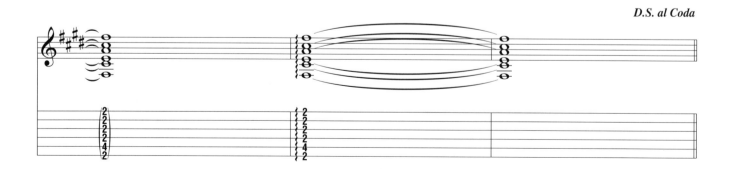

Additional Lyrics

2. A year has passed since I wrote my note.
   I should have known this right from the start.
   Only hope can keep me together.
   Love can mend your life, but love can break your heart.

3. Woke up this morning, I don't believe what I saw,
   Hundred billion bottles washed up on the shore.
   Seems I never noticed being alone.
   Hundred billion castaways, looking for a home.

Mississippi Queen

Words and Music by Leslie West, Felix Pappalardi, Corky Laing and David Rea

Intro
Moderately ♩ = 140

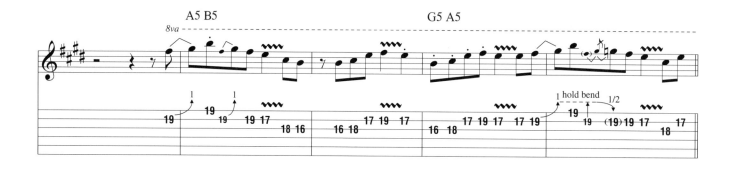

Chorus

Mis - sis - sip - pi Queen, _____ do you know _____

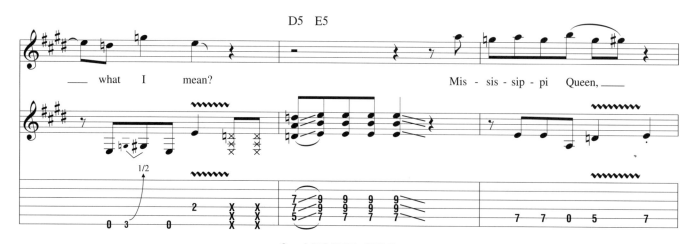

_____ what I mean? Mis - sis - sip - pi Queen, _____

she moved ___ bet - ter on wine. While the rest of them dudes was a

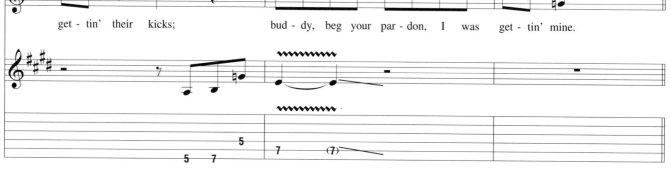

get - tin' their kicks; bud - dy, beg your par - don, I was get - tin' mine.

Chorus

Mis - sis - sip - pi Queen, ___ if you know ___

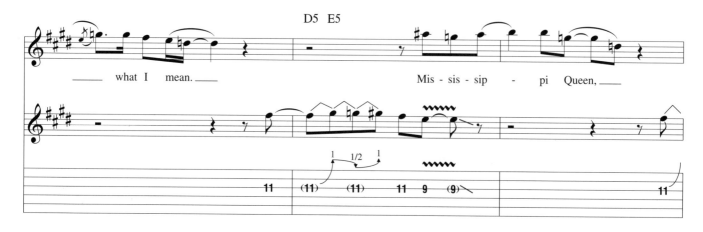

___ what I mean. ___ Mis - sis - sip - pi Queen, ___

she taught me ev - 'ry - thing.

2. This la -

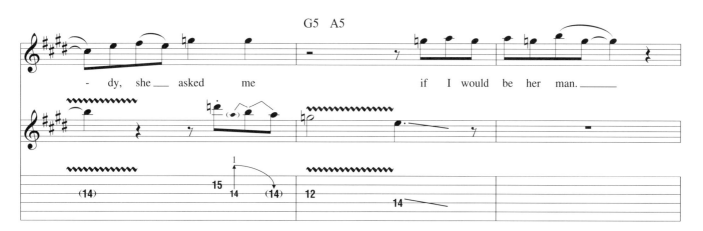

- dy, she asked me if I would be her man.

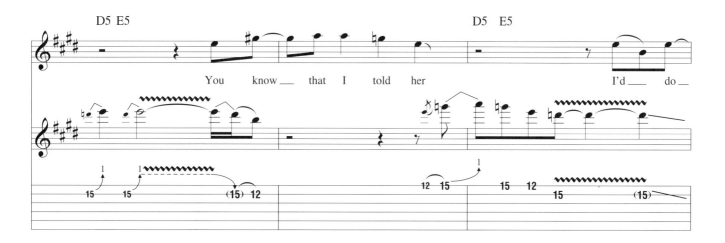

You know that I told her I'd do

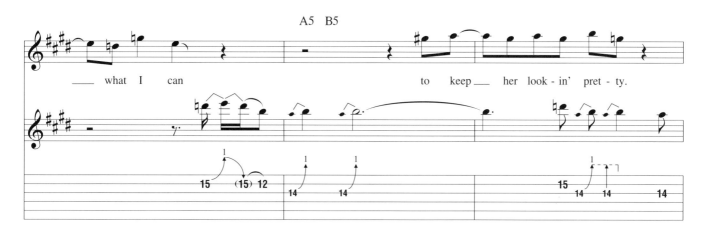

what I can to keep her look - in' pret - ty.

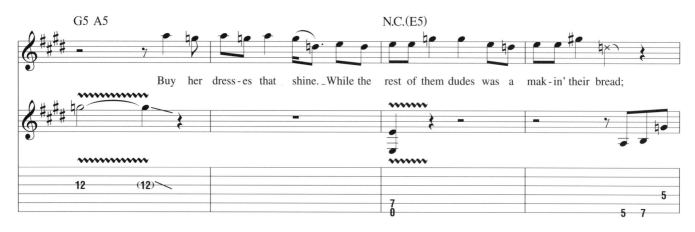

Buy her dress-es that   shine._While the   rest of them dudes was a   mak-in' their bread;

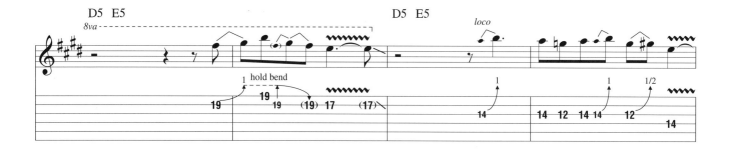

bud-dy, beg your par-don, I   was   los-in' mine.

Guitar Solo
D5 E5

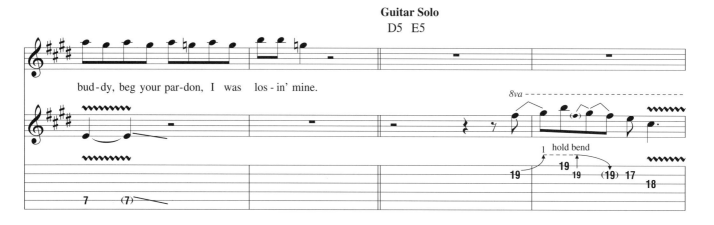

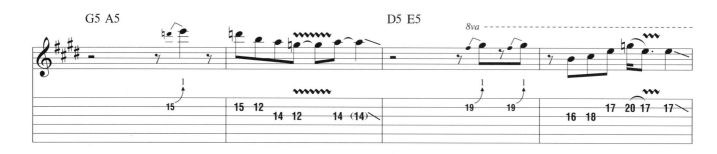

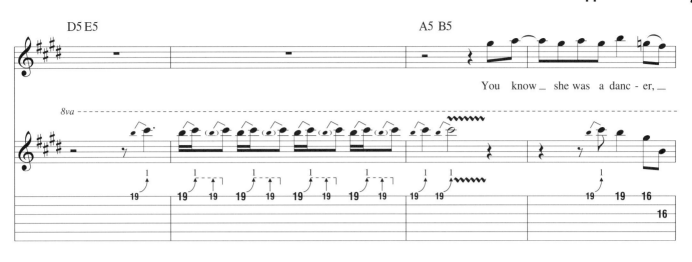

You know ___ she was a danc - er, ___

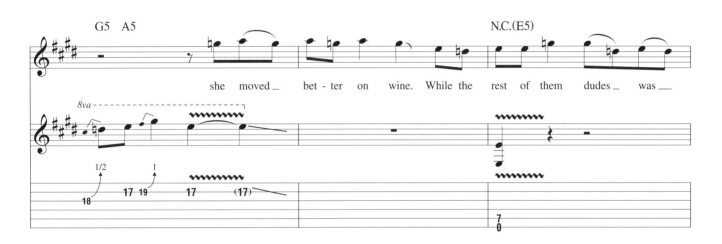

she moved ___ bet - ter on wine. While the rest of them dudes ___ was ___

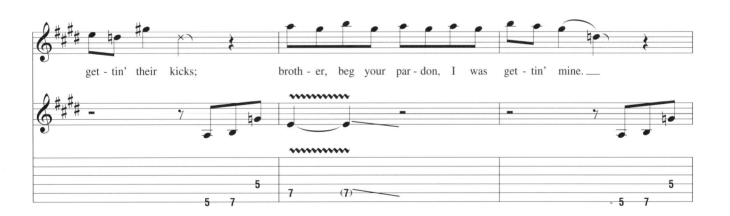

get - tin' their kicks; broth - er, beg your par - don, I was get - tin' mine. ___

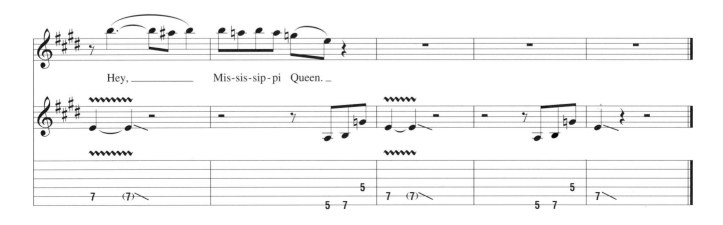

Hey, _____ Mis - sis - sip - pi Queen. ___

Money for Nothing

Words and Music by Mark Knopfler and Sting

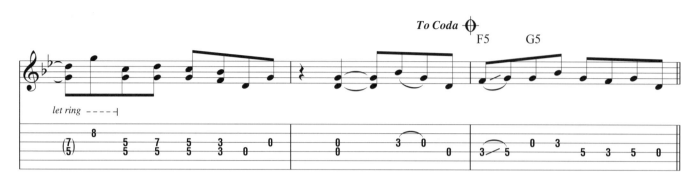

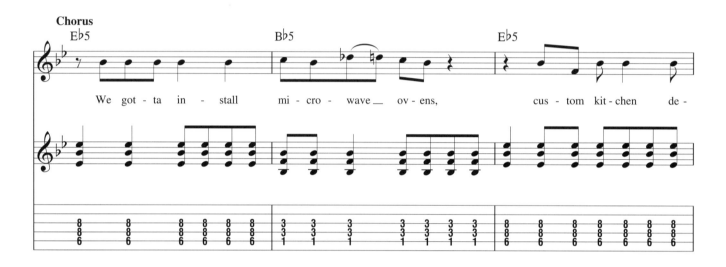

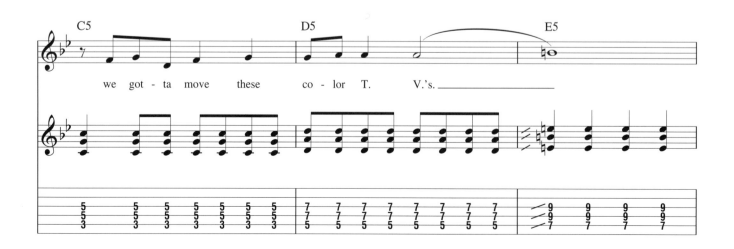

Outro

Additional Lyrics

3. I should have learned to play the guitar,
I should have learned to play them drums.
Look at that mama, she got it stickin' in the cameraman.
We could have some fun.
And he's up there, what's that? Hawaiian noises?
He's bangin' on the bongos like a chimpanzee.
Oh, that ain't workin', that's the way to do it.
Get your money for nothing, get your chicks for free.

Oh, Pretty Woman

Words and Music by Roy Orbison and Bill Dees

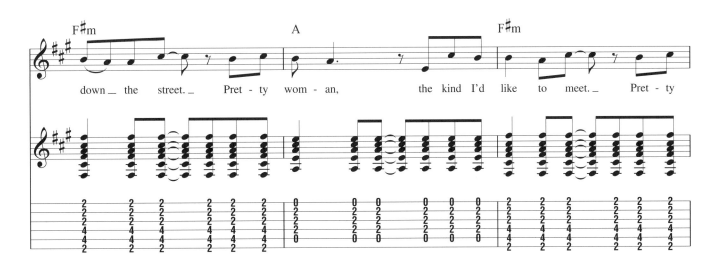

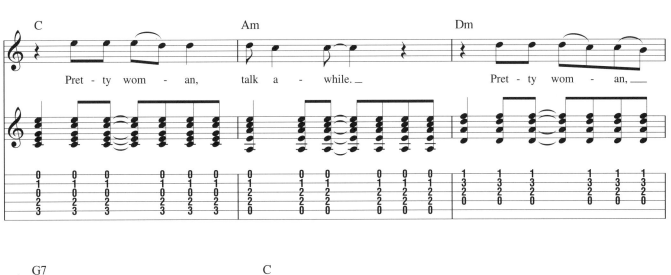

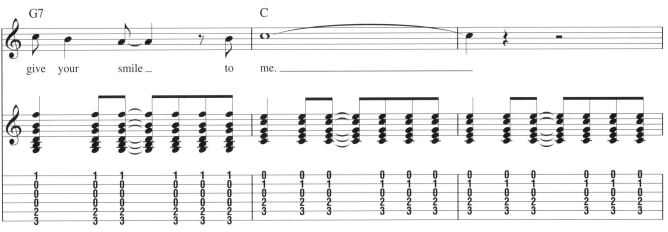

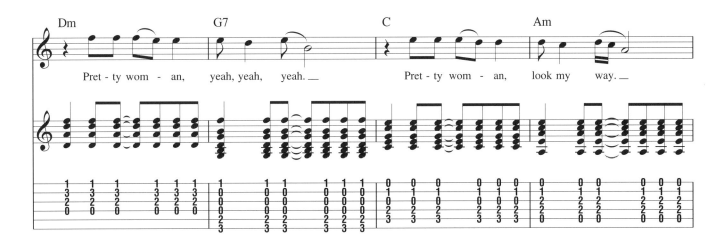

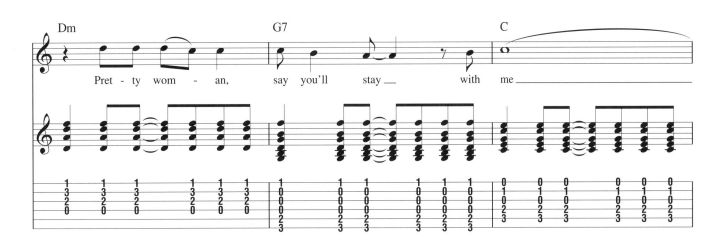

Additional Lyrics

2. Pretty woman, won't you pardon me?
    Pretty woman, I couldn't help but see;
    Pretty woman, that you look lovely as can be.
    Are you lonely just like me?

Proud Mary

Words and Music by John Fogerty

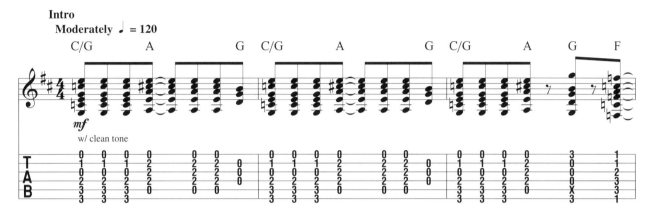

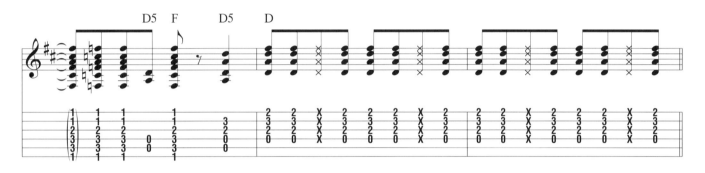

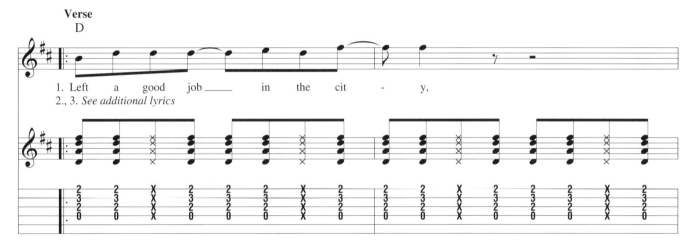

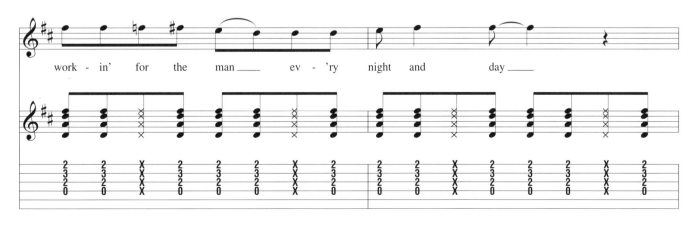

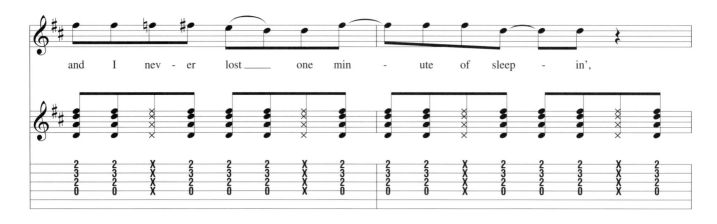

and I nev - er lost ____ one min - ute of sleep - in',

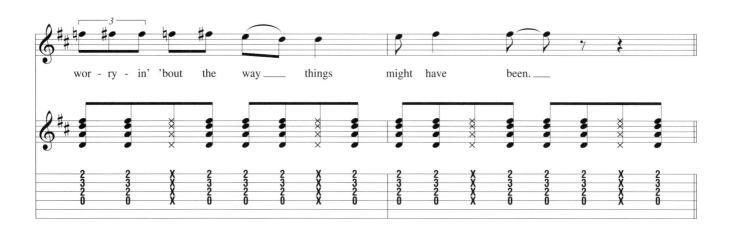

wor - ry - in' 'bout the way ____ things might have been. ____

Pre-Chorus

2nd & 3rd times, substitute Fill 1

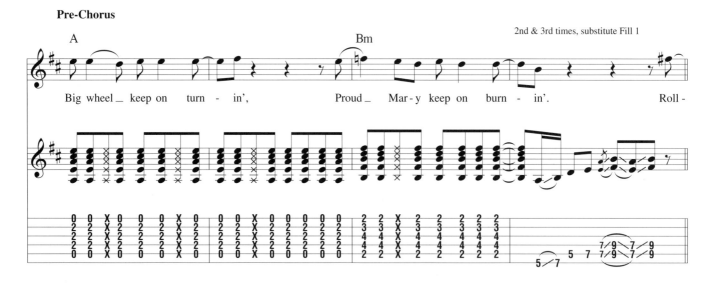

Big wheel _ keep on turn - in', Proud _ Mar - y keep on burn - in'. Roll -

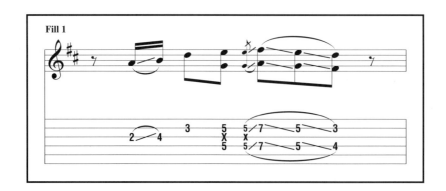

Fill 1

Chorus

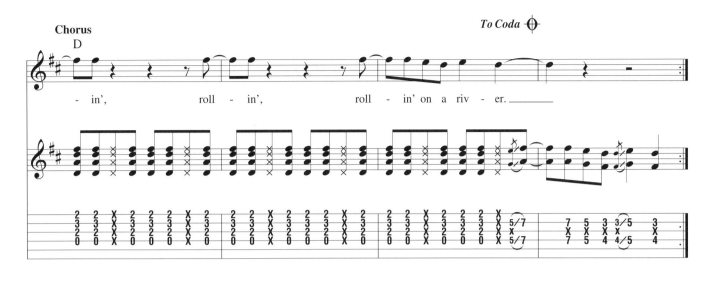

-in', roll - in', roll - in' on a riv - er.

Interlude

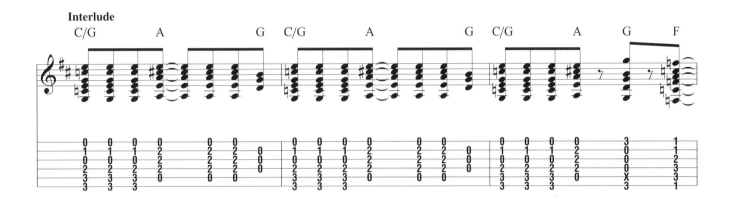

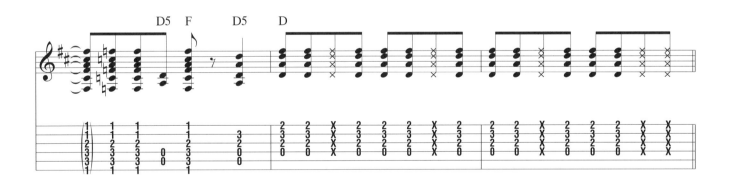

Guitar Solo

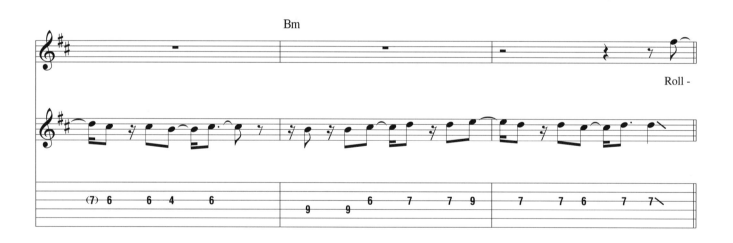

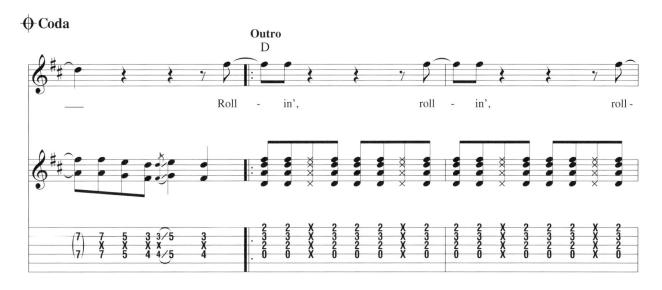

Additional Lyrics

2. Cleaned a lot of plates in Memphis,
   Pumped a lot of pain down in New Orleans,
   But I never saw the good side of the city
   Till I hitched a ride on a riverboat queen.

3. If you come down to the river,
   Bet you're gonna find some people who live.
   You don't have to worry 'cause you have no money,
   People on the river are happy to give.

Rebel, Rebel

Words and Music by David Bowie

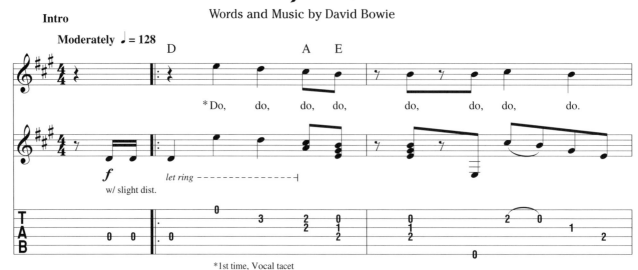

*1st time, Vocal tacet

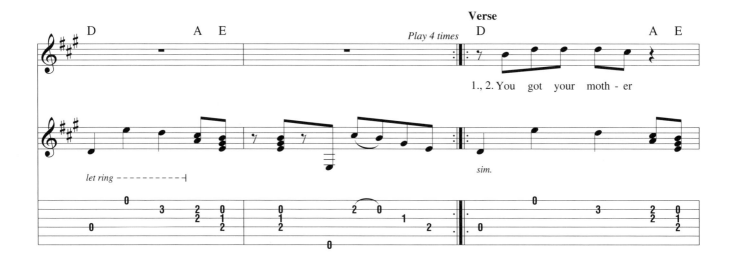

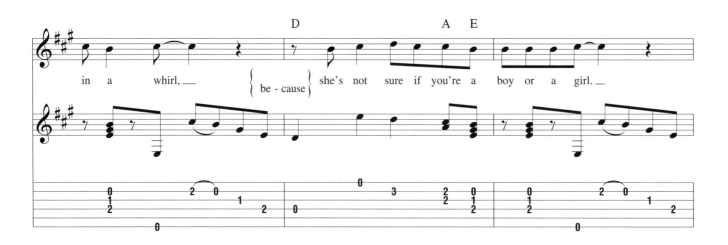

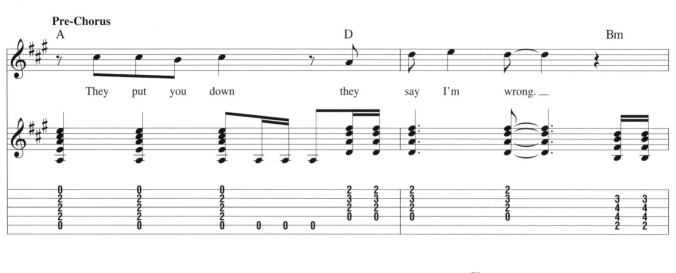

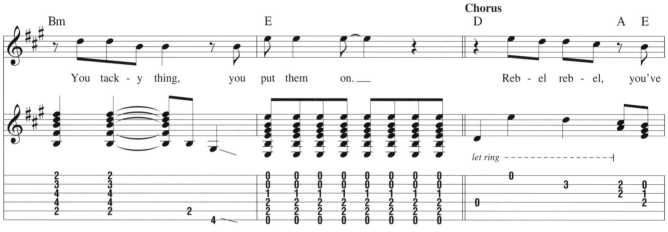

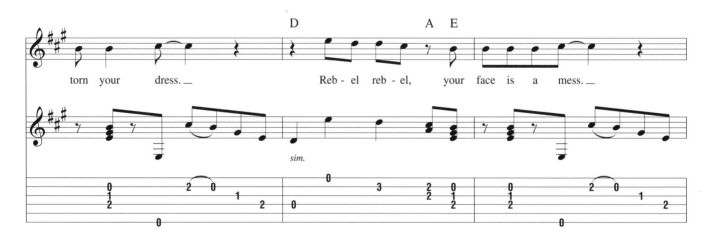

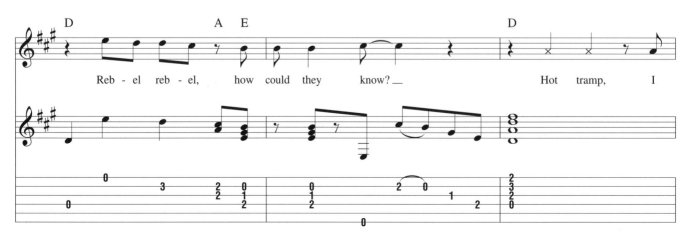

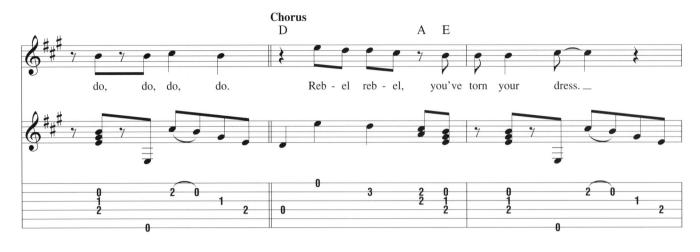

do, do, do, do. Reb - el reb - el, you've torn your dress.

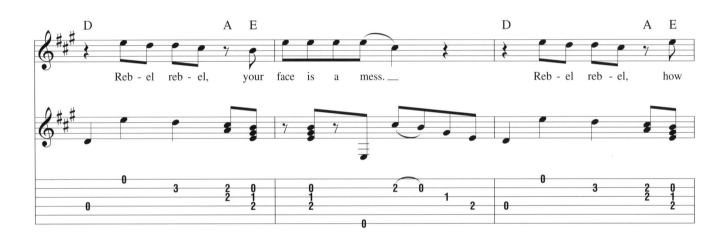

Reb - el reb - el, your face is a mess. Reb - el reb - el, how

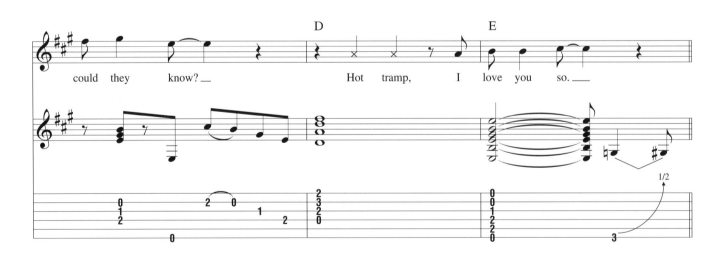

could they know? Hot tramp, I love you so.

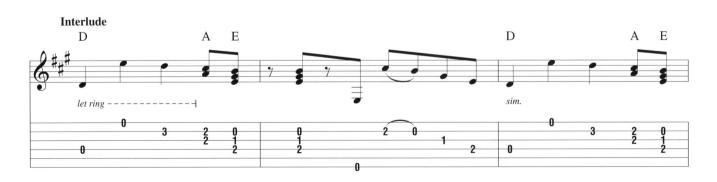

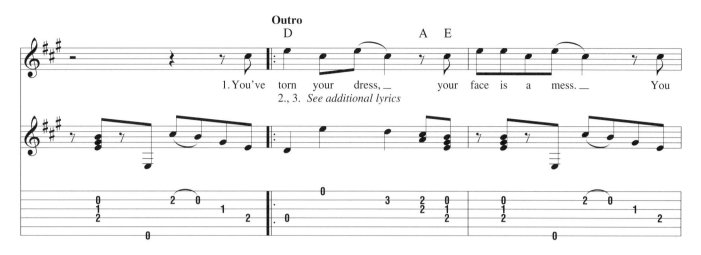

Outro

1. You've torn your dress, ___ your face is a mess. ___ You
2., 3. *See additional lyrics*

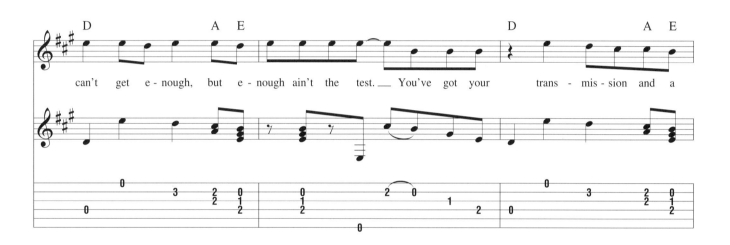

can't get e-nough, but e-nough ain't the test. ___ You've got your trans-mis-sion and a

Play 3 times and fade

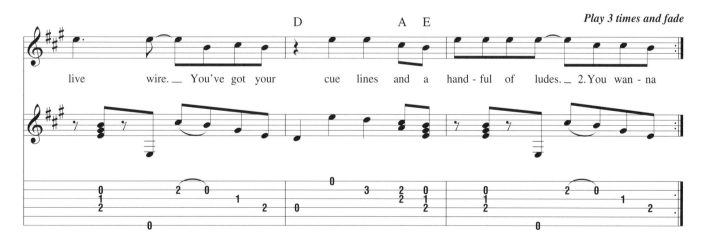

live wire. ___ You've got your cue lines and a hand-ful of ludes. ___ 2. You wan-na

Additional Lyrics

Outro 2. You wanna be there when they count up the dudes.
And I love your dress.
You're a juvenile success,
'Cause your face is a mess.

Outro 3. So how could they know,
I said, how could they know?
So what you wanna know, Calamity's child?
Ch-child, ah child, oh where d'ya wanna go?

Refugee

Words and Music by Tom Petty and Mike Campbell

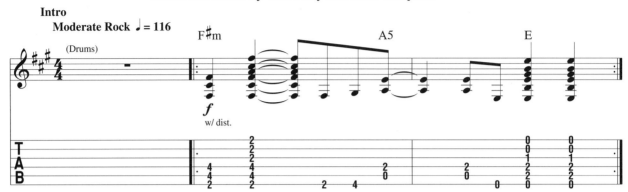

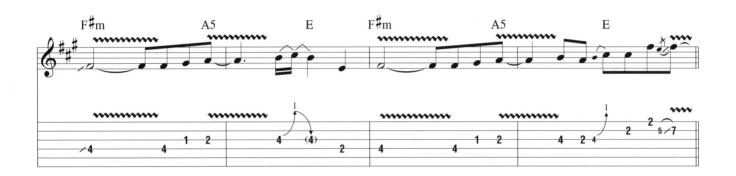

1. We got some-thin', we both know it, we don't talk too much a-bout ___ it.

2.,3. *See additional lyrics*

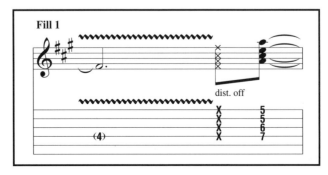

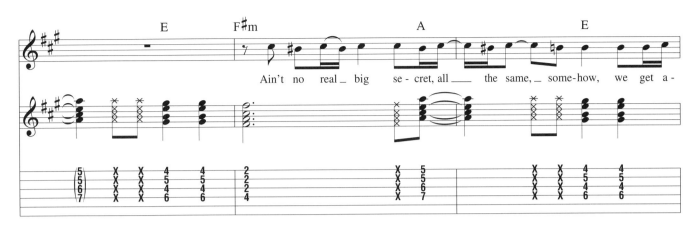

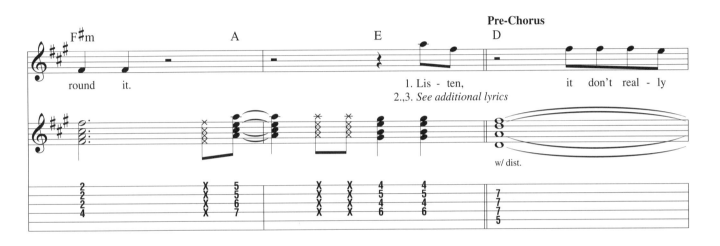

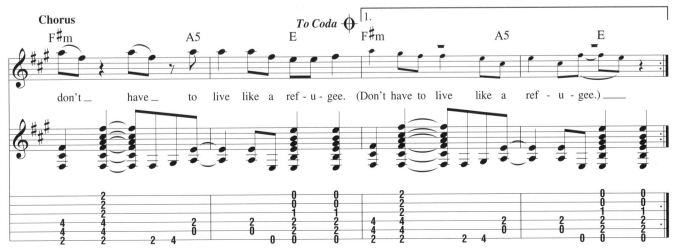

Organ/Guitar Solo

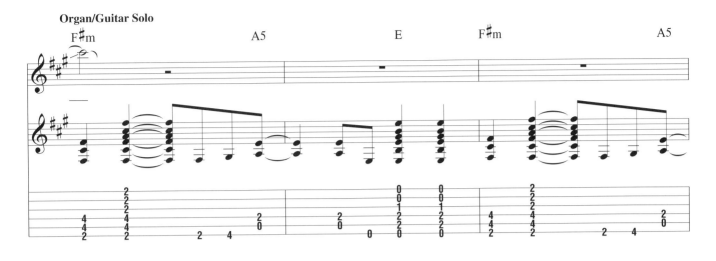

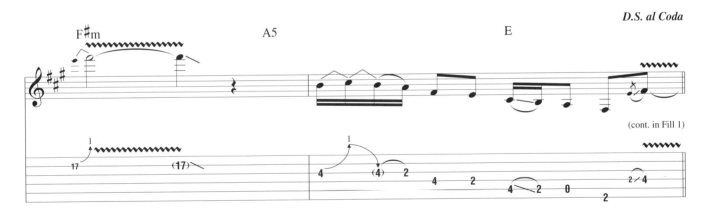

D.S. al Coda

(cont. in Fill 1)

Coda

No, you don't have ___ to

(Don't have to live like a ref - u - gee.) ___

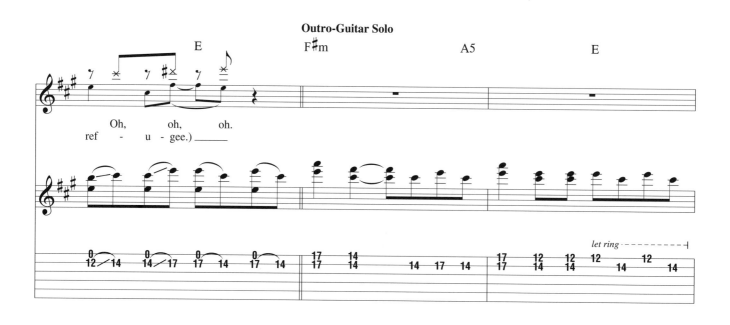

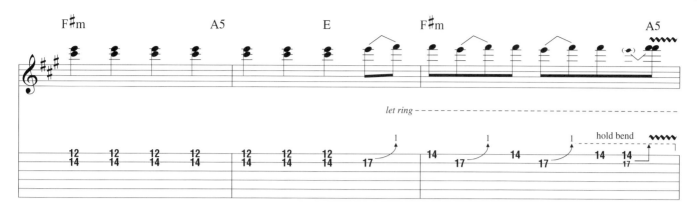

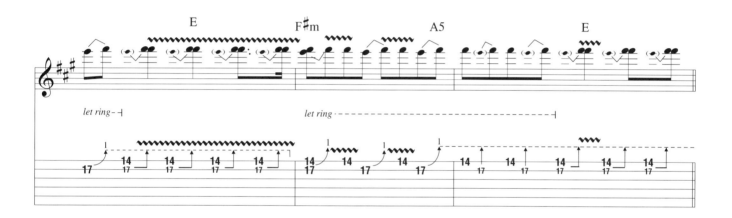

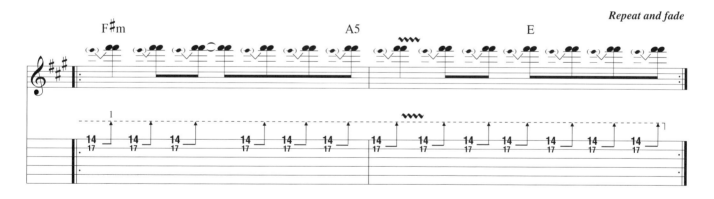

Additional Lyrics

2. Somewhere, somehow, somebody must have
   Kicked you around some.
   Tell me why you wanna lay there,
   Revel in your abandon.

Pre-Chorus 2. Honey, it don't make no diff'rence to me.
   Baby, ev'rybody's had to fight to be free.

3. Somewhere, somehow, somebody must have
   Kicked you around some.
   Who knows? Maybe you were kidnapped,
   Tied up, taken away and held for ransom.

Pre-Chorus 3. Honey, it don't really matter to me.
   Baby, ev'rybody's had to fight to be free.

Rock and Roll All Nite

Words and Music by Paul Stanley and Gene Simmons

Tune down 1/2 step:
(low to high) Eb–Ab–Db–Gb–Bb–Eb

Intro

Moderately fast Rock ♩ = 142

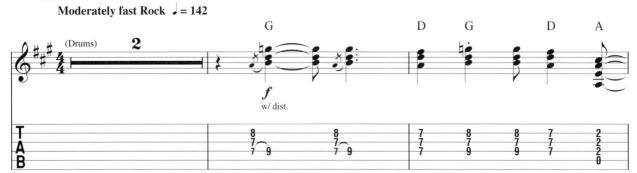

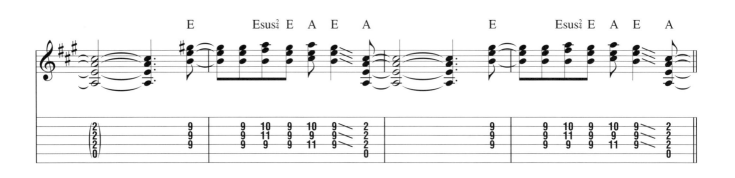

Verse

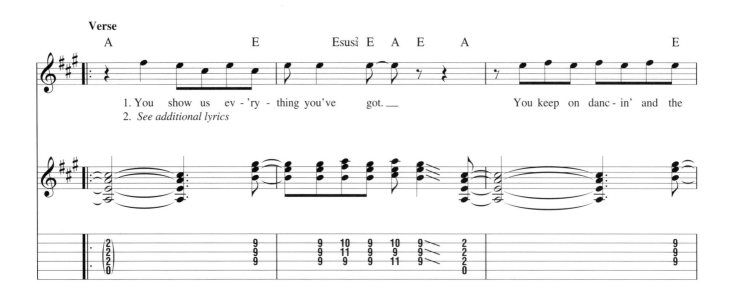

1. You show us ev-'ry-thing you've got. ___ You keep on danc-in' and the
2. *See additional lyrics*

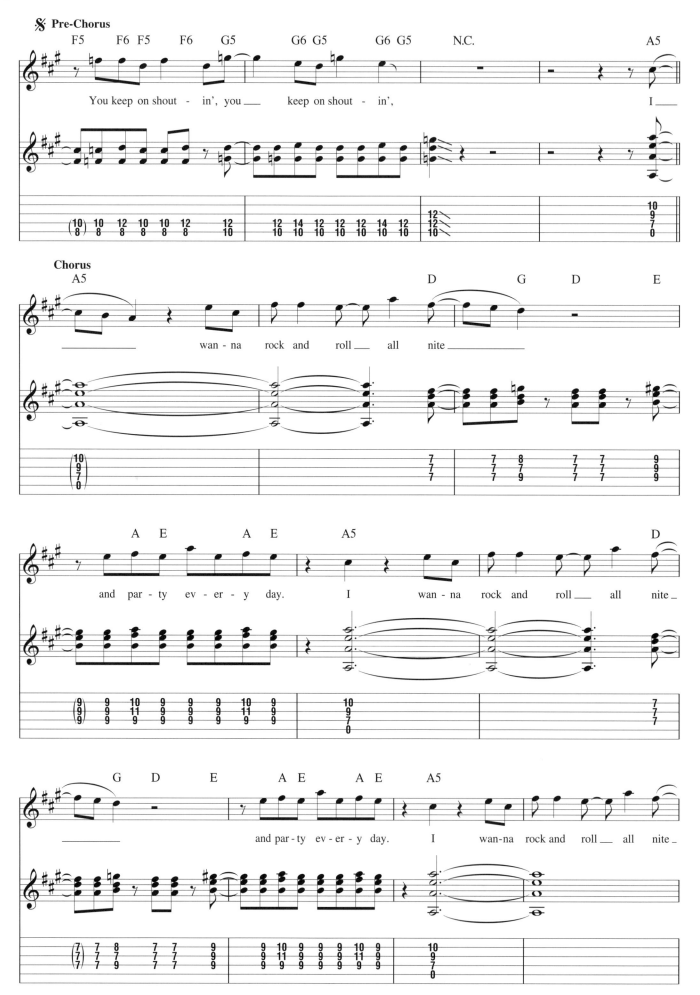

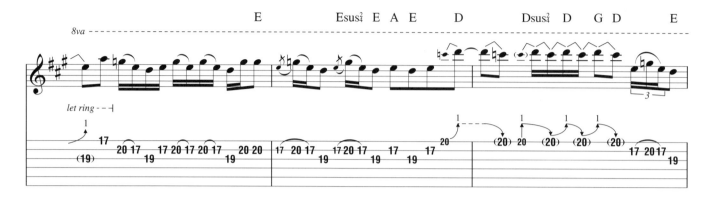

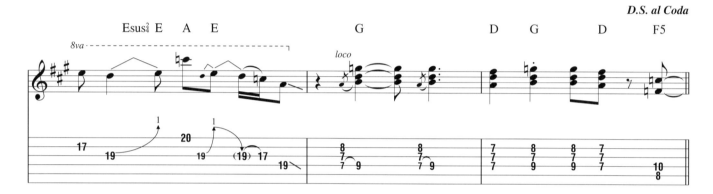

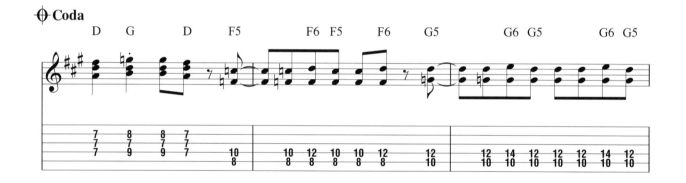

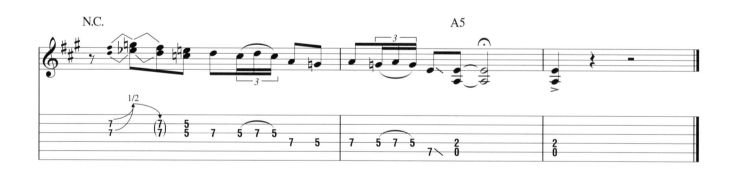

Additional Lyrics

2. You keep on sayin' you'll be mine for awhile.
   You're looking fancy and I like your style.
   And you drive us wild; we'll drive you crazy.
   And you show us ev'rything you've got.
   Well, baby, baby, that's quite a lot.
   And you drive us wild; we'll drive you crazy.

R.O.C.K. in the U.S.A. (A Salute to '60s Rock)

Words and Music by John Mellencamp

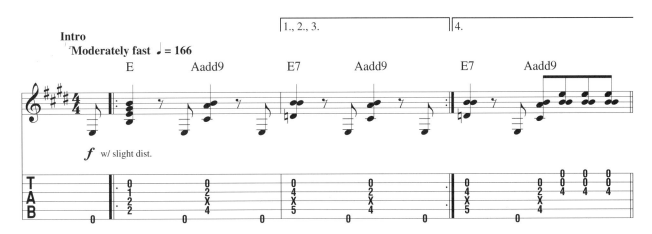

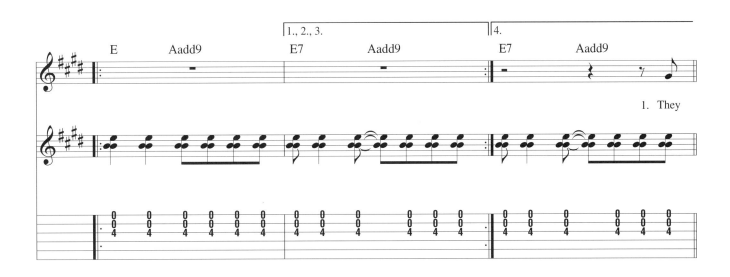

1. They

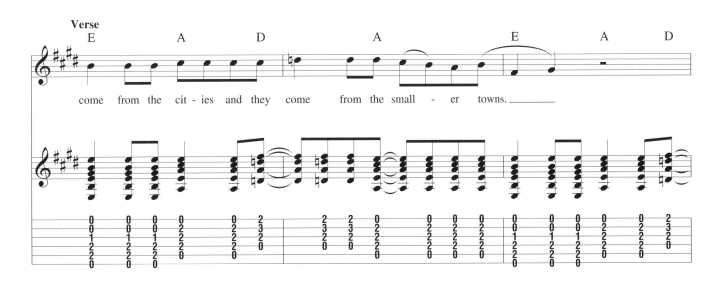

come from the cit - ies and they come from the small - er towns.

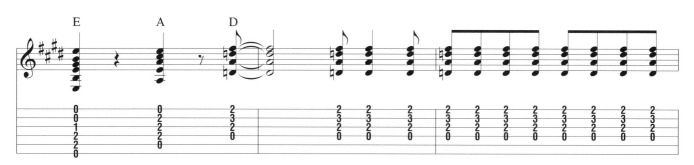

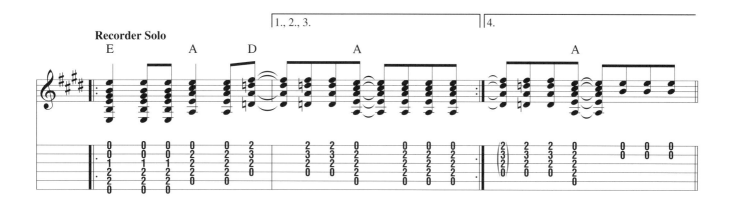

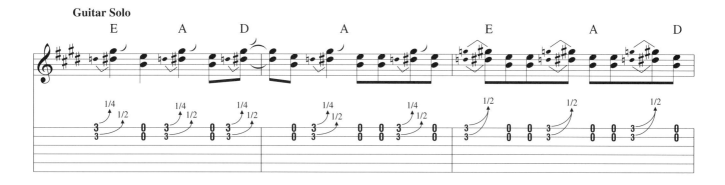

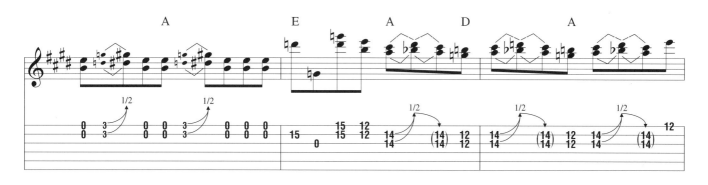

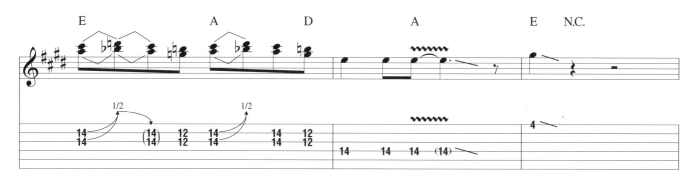

Rock This Town

Words and Music by Brian Setzer

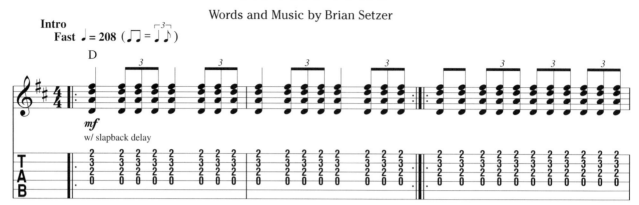

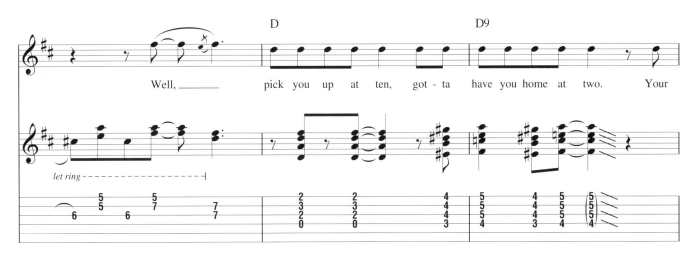

Well, _____ pick you up at ten, got-ta have you home at two. Your

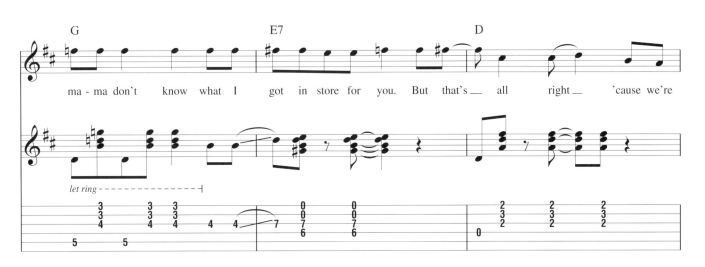

ma-ma don't know what I got in store for you. But that's __ all right __ 'cause we're

Interlude

look-in' as cool as can be. _____

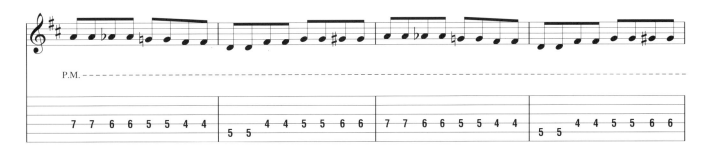

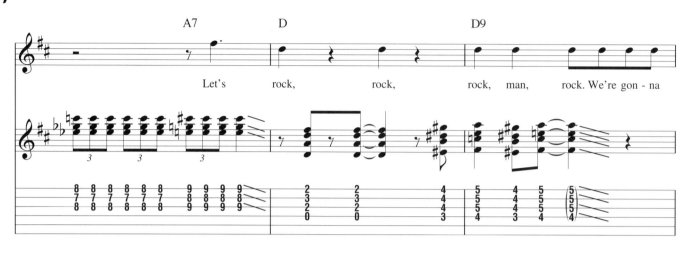

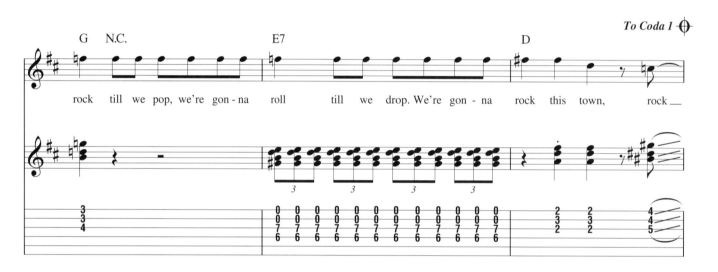

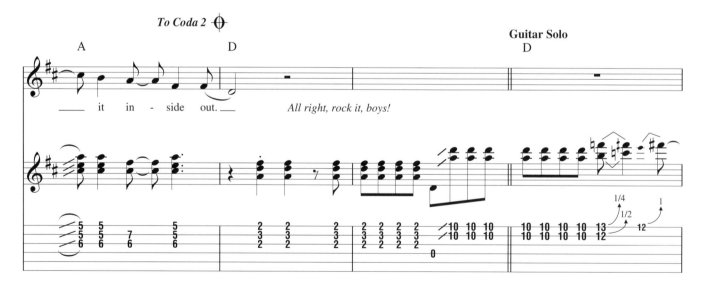

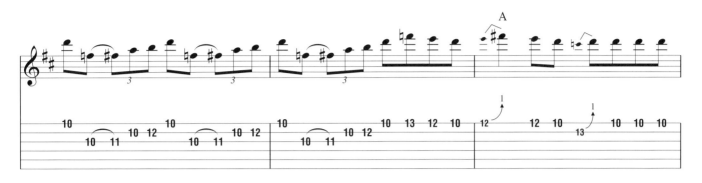

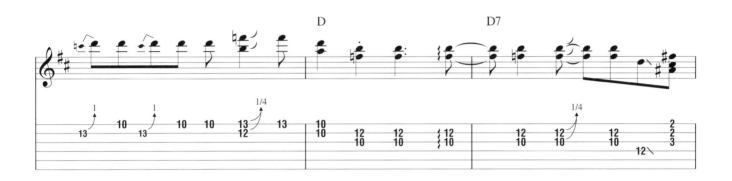

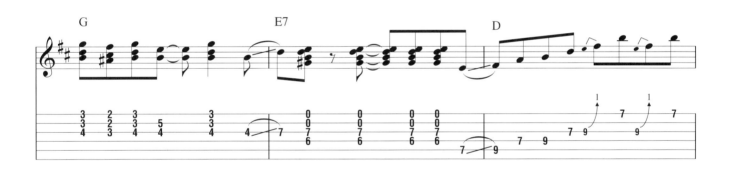

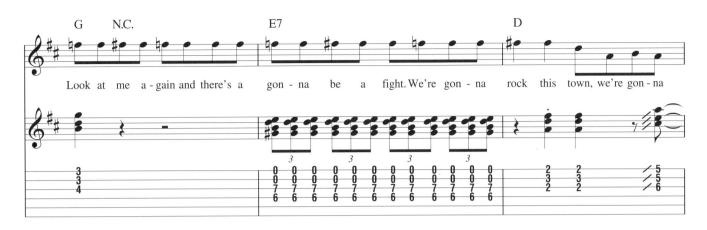

Look at me a-gain and there's a gon - na be a fight. We're gon - na rock this town, we're gon - na

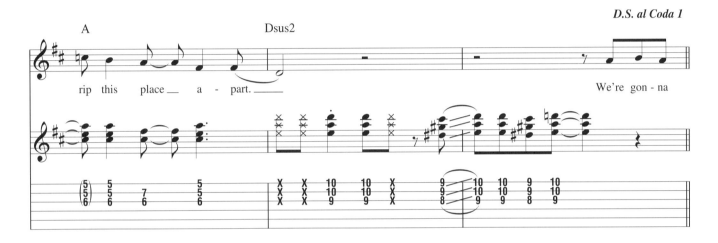

rip this place ___ a - part. ___

D.S. al Coda 1

We're gon - na

Coda 1

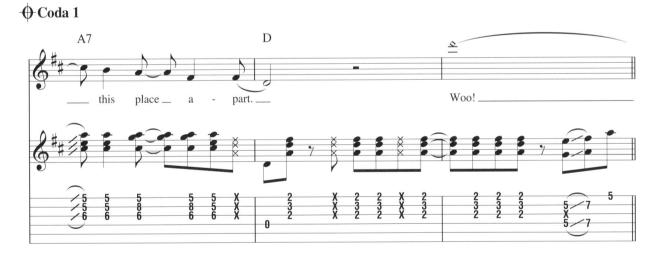

___ this place ___ a - part. ___

Woo! ___

Guitar Solo

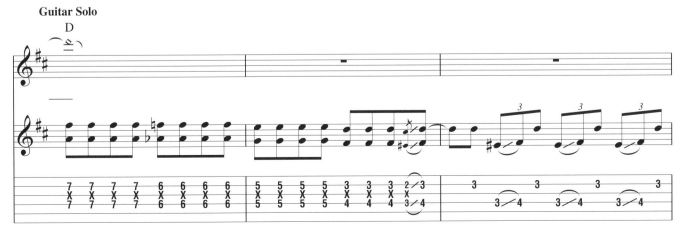

⊕ Coda 2

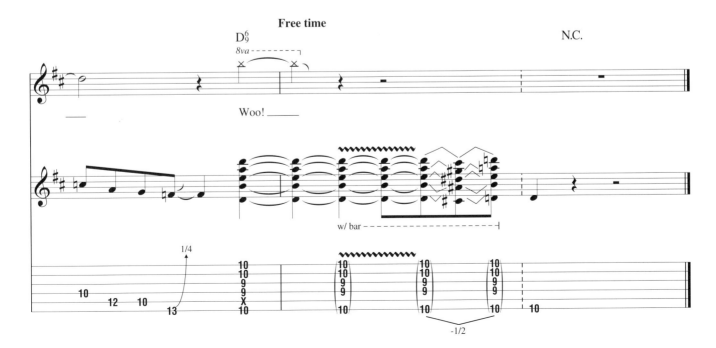

Rock'n Me

Words and Music by Steve Miller

⊕ Coda

Outro-Chorus

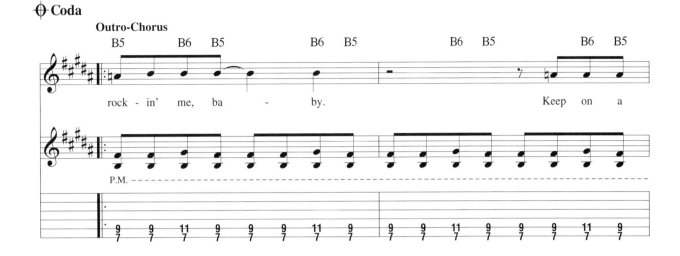

rock - in' me, ba - by. Keep on a

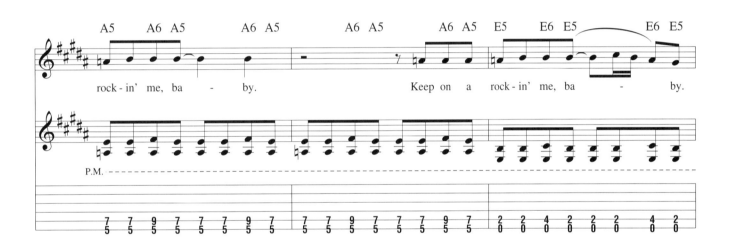

rock - in' me, ba - by. Keep on a rock - in' me, ba - by.

Repeat and fade

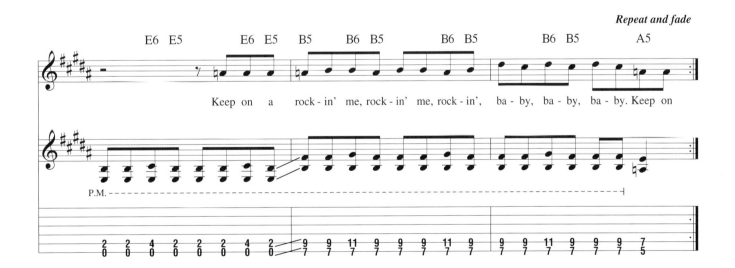

Keep on a rock - in' me, rock - in' me, rock - in', ba - by, ba - by, ba - by. Keep on

Additional Lyrics

3. Don't get suspicious, now don't be suspicious,
   Babe, you know you are a friend of mine.
   And you know that it's true, that all the things that I do
   Are gonna come back to you in your sweet time.
   I went from Phoenix, Arizona, all the way to Tacoma,
   Philadelphia, Atlanta, L.A.
   Northern California where the girls are warm,
   So I could hear my sweet, mm, baby say.

Rocky Mountain Way

Words and Music by Joe Walsh, Joe Vitale, Ken Passarelli and Rocke Grace

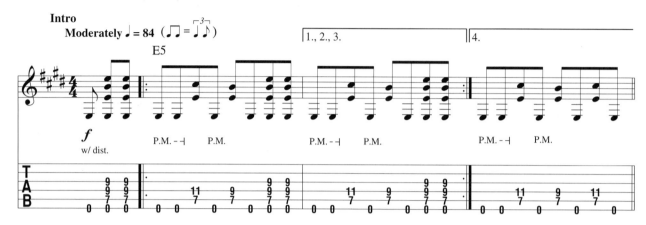

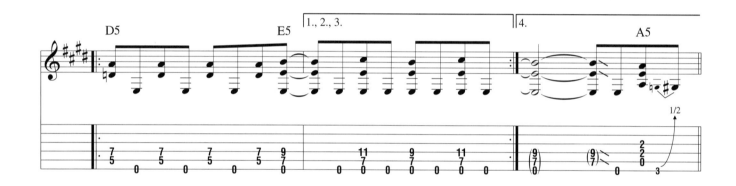

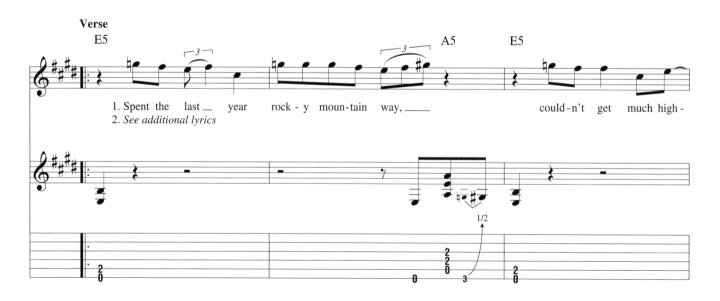

1. Spent the last year rock-y moun-tain way, _____ could-n't get much high-
2. *See additional lyrics*

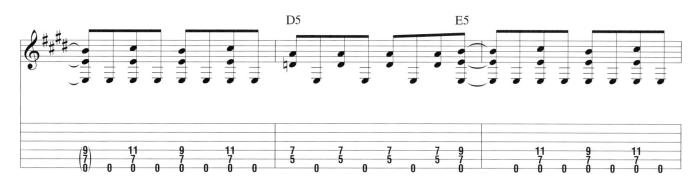

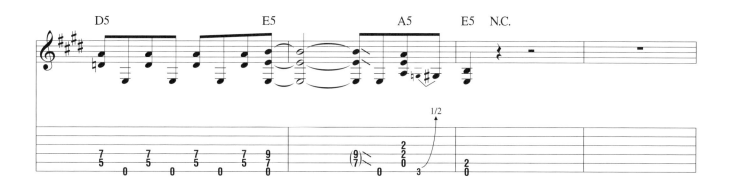

Guitar Solo

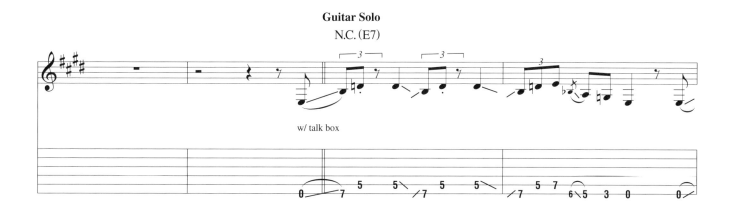

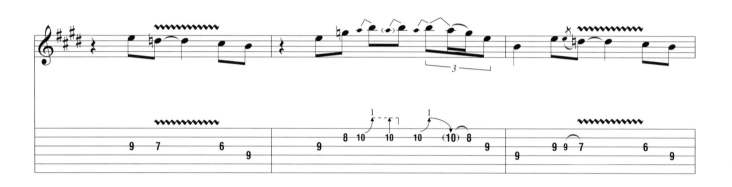

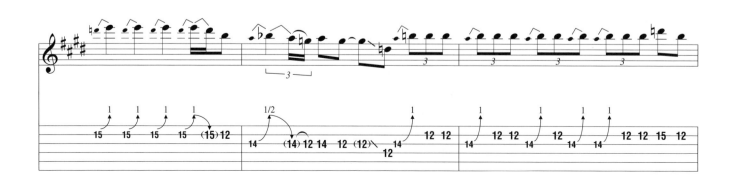

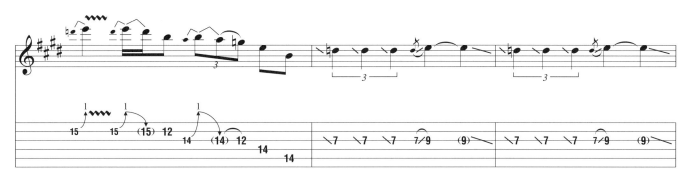

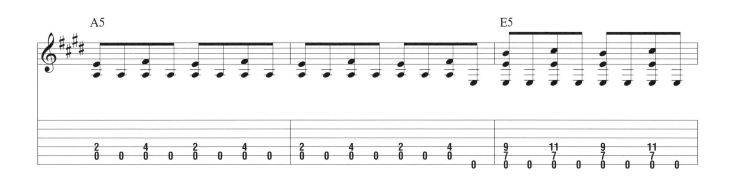

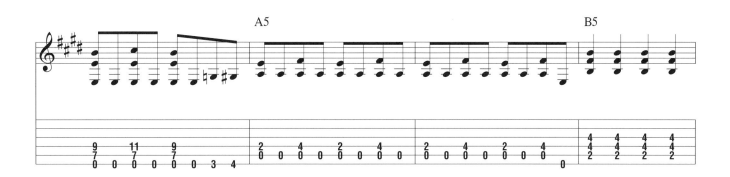

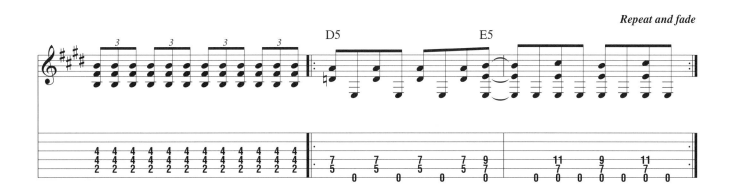

Additional Lyrics

2. Well, he's tellin' us this and he's tellin' us that,
   Changes it ev'ry day;
   Says it doesn't matter.
   Bases are loaded and Casey's at bat,
   Playin' it play by play;
   Time to change the batter.

Shattered

Words and Music by Mick Jagger and Keith Richards

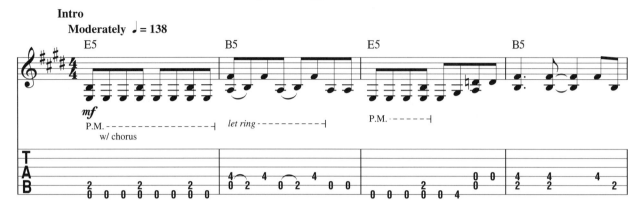

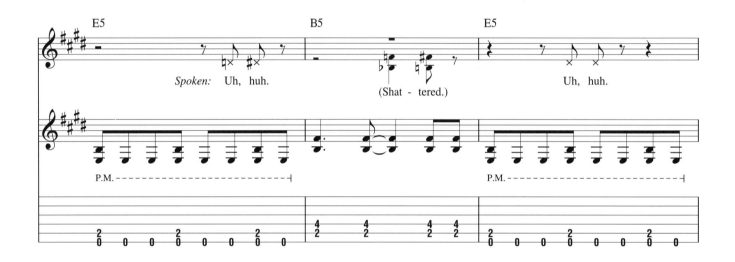

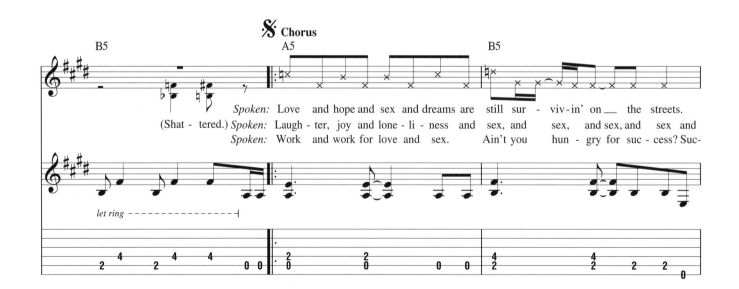

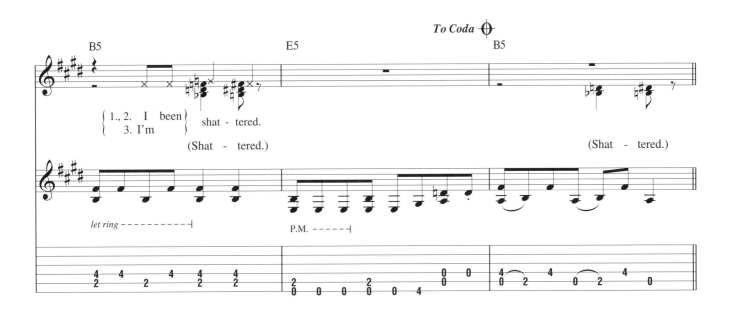

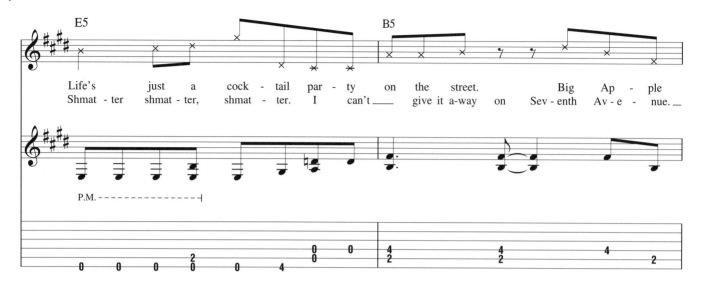

Life's just a cock - tail par - ty on the street. Big Ap - ple
Shmat - ter shmat - ter, shmat - ter. I can't__ give it a - way on Sev - enth Av - e - nue.__

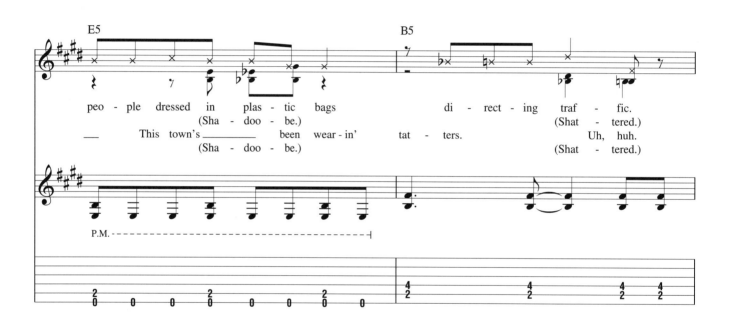

peo - ple dressed in plas - tic bags di - rect - ing traf - fic.
(Sha - doo - be.) (Shat - tered.)
__ This town's__ been wear - in' tat - ters. Uh, huh.
(Sha - doo - be.) (Shat - tered.)

2nd time, D.S. al Coda

Coda

Some kind a fash - ion.
(Sha - doo - be.) (Shat - tered.)

(Sha - doo - be.) (Shat - tered.)

Does it mat - ter?__
(Shat - tered.)

Guitar Solo

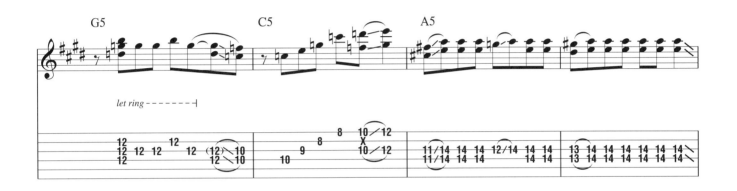

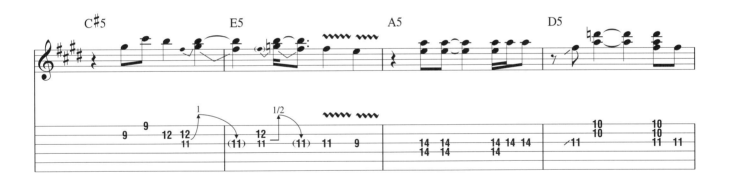

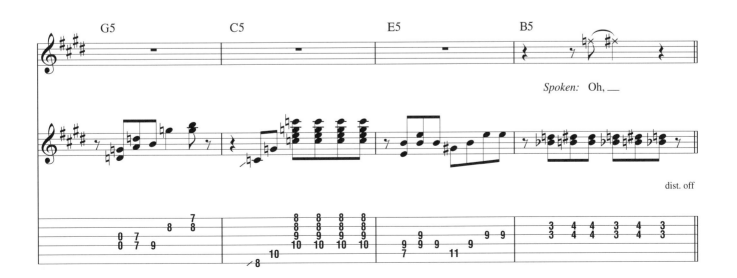

Chorus

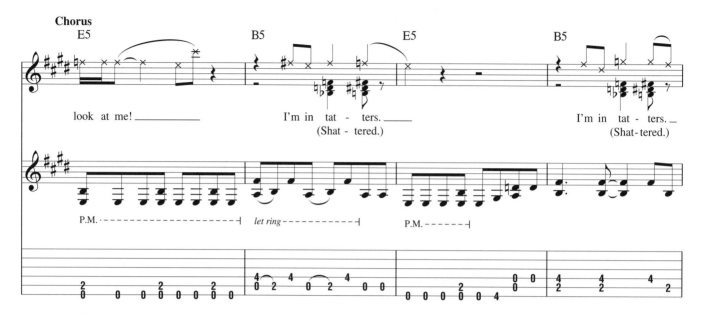

look at me! _____   I'm in tat - ters. _____   I'm in tat - ters. __
                        (Shat - tered.)   (Shat-tered.)

Look at me! _   I been shat - tered.   Yeah!   (Shat - tered.)
                (Shat - tered)

Verse

3. *Spoken:* Pride and joy and greed and sex,   that's what makes our town the best. __   Pride and joy and dirt - y dreams are

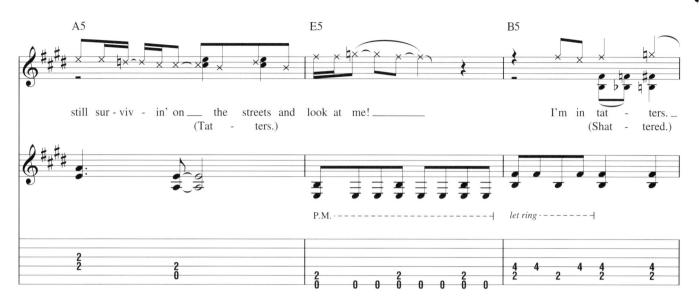

still sur - viv - in' on ___ the streets and look at me! ___
(Tat - ters.)

I'm in tat - ters. ___
(Shat - tered.)

Outro

___ Yeah! ___

I been bat - tered.
(Shat - tered.)

What does it mat - ter? ___
(Shat - tered.)
See additional lyrics

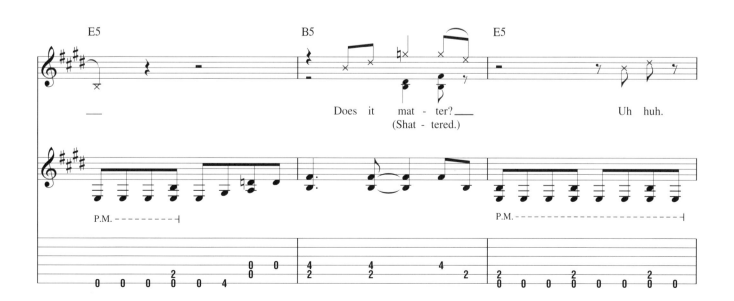

Does it mat - ter? ___
(Shat - tered.)

Uh huh.

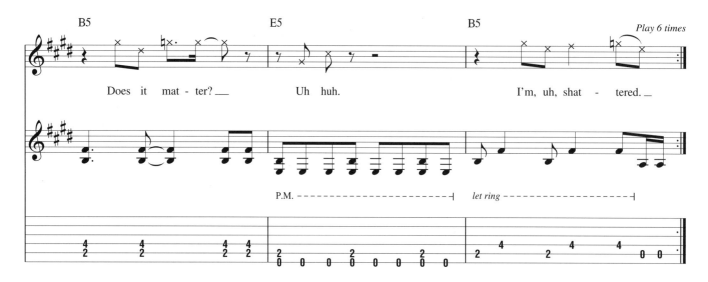

Additional Lyrics

Outro Mm. I'm shattered. Huh! Sha-doo-bee. Shattered.
Huh! Sha-doo-bee. Shattered.
Sha-doo-bee. (Shattered. Shattered.)
Don't you know the crime rate's goin' up, up, up, up, up?
To live in this town you must be tough, tough, tough, tough, tough, tough, tough.
(Shattered. Shattered.) We got rats on the West Side, bedbugs uptown.
What a mess! This town's in tatters.
I been shattered. My brain's been battered,
Splattered all over Manhattan. Uh, huh.
What say? Sha-doo-bee. Uh, huh.
This town's full of money grabbers.
Go ahead! Bite the Big Apple. Don't mind the maggots!
Uh, huh. (Shattered.) Sha-doo-bee. My brain's been battered!
My fam'ly come around 'n' flatter, flatter, flatter, flatter, flatter, flatter, flatter.
Pile it up! (Shattered.) Pile it up. (Sha-doo-bee.)
Pile it high on the platter!

Smoke on the Water

Words and Music by Ritchie Blackmore, Ian Gillan, Roger Glover, Jon Lord and Ian Paice

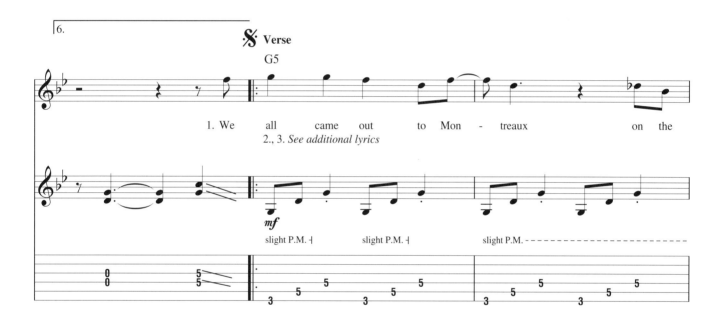

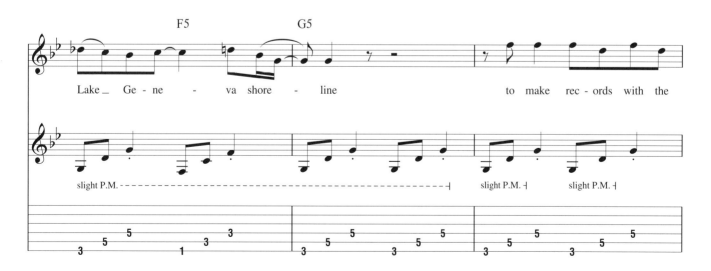

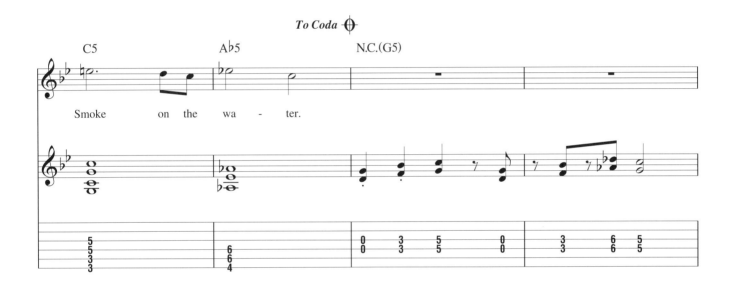

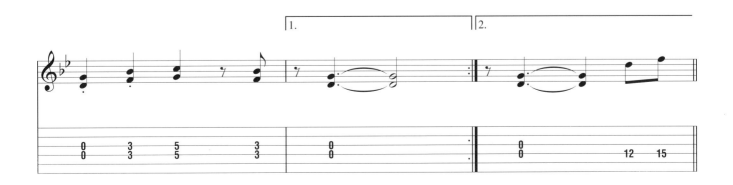

Guitar Solo

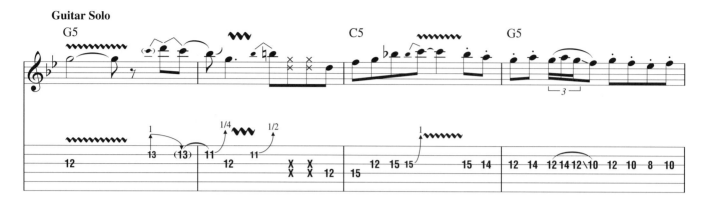

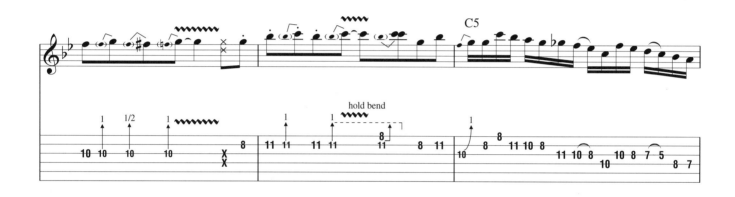

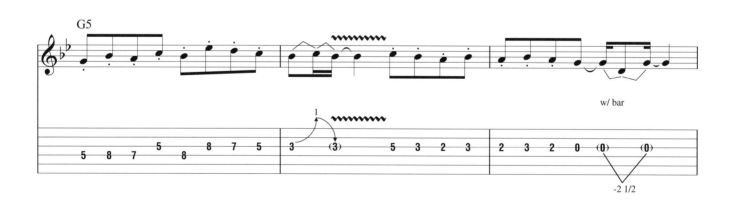

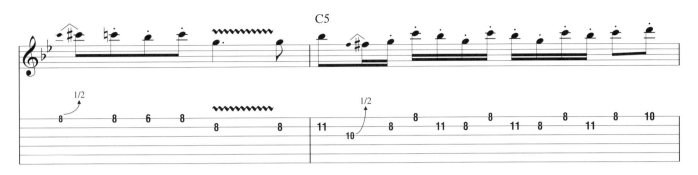

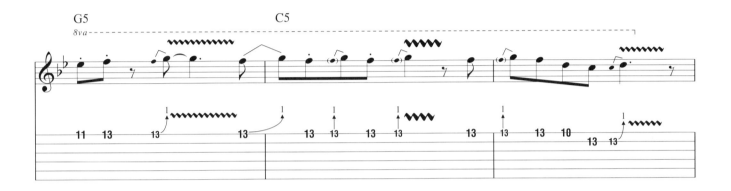

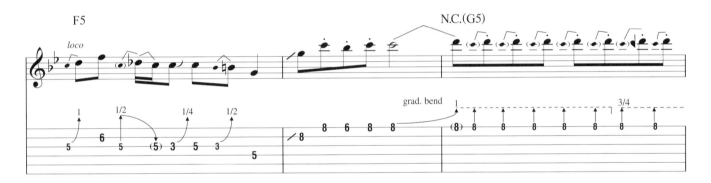

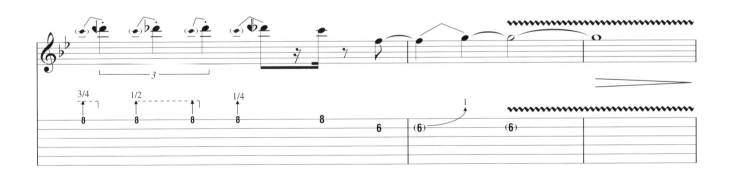

Coda

Outro-Organ Solo

Begin fade

Fade out

Additional Lyrics

2. They burned down the gambling house,
   It died with an awful sound.
   A Funky Claude was running in and out,
   Pulling kids out the ground.
   When it all was over, we had to find another place.
   But Swiss time was running out;
   It seemed we would lose the race.

3. We ended up at the Grand Hotel,
   It was empty, cold and bare.
   But with the Rolling truck Stones thing just outside,
   Making our music there.
   With a few red lights, a few old beds
   We made a place to sweat.
   No matter what we get out of this,
   I know, I know we'll never forget.

Summer of '69

Words and Music by Bryan Adams and Jim Vallance

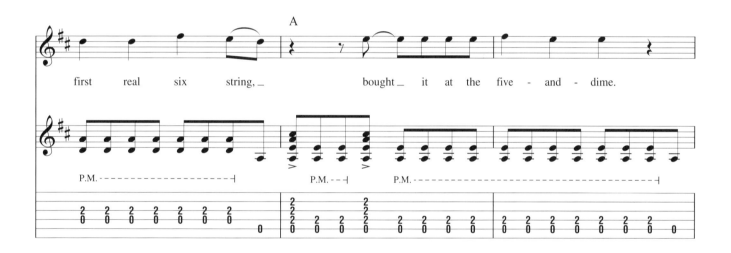

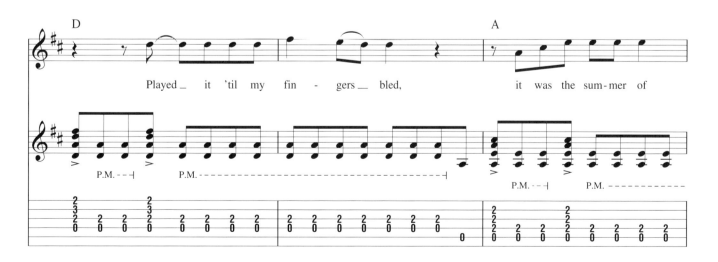

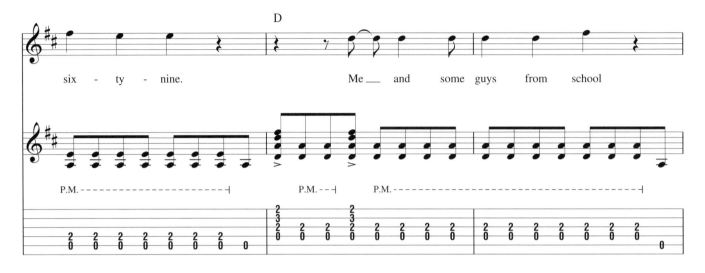

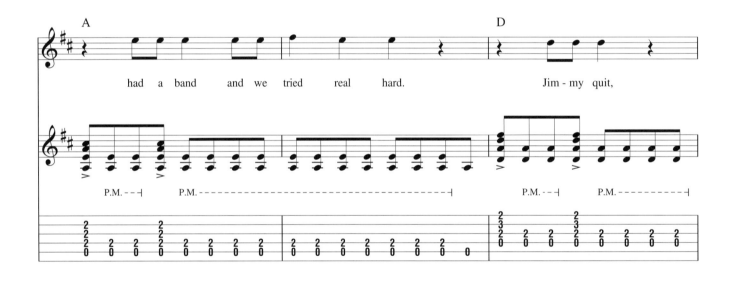

%. Pre-Chorus

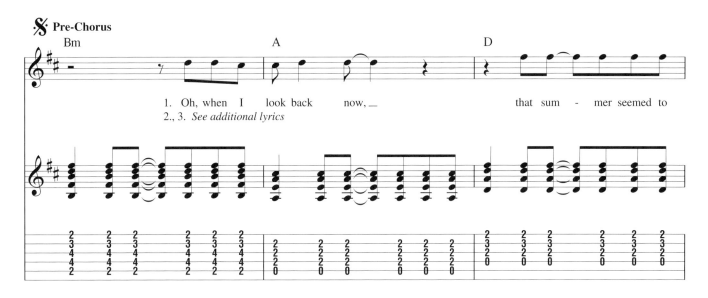

1. Oh, when I look back now, _____ that sum - mer seemed to
2., 3. *See additional lyrics*

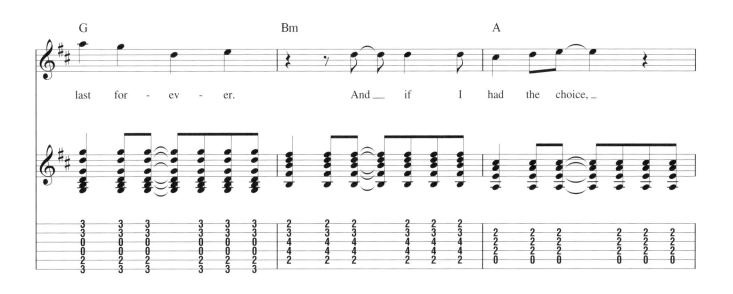

last for - ev - er. And _____ if I had the choice, _____

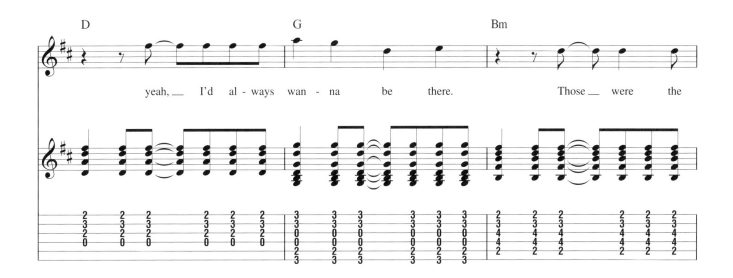

yeah, _____ I'd al - ways wan - na be there. Those _____ were the

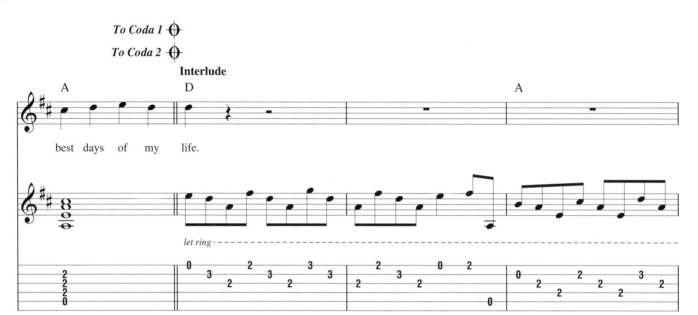

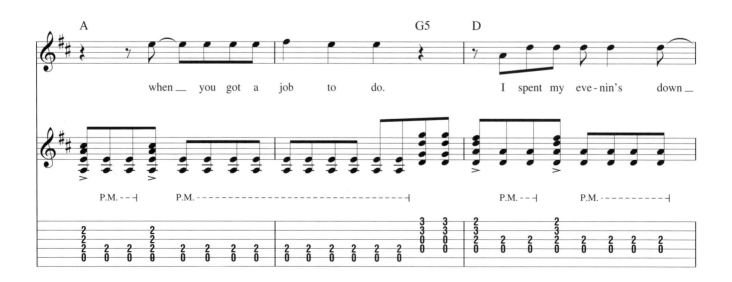

D.S. al Coda 1

at the drive - in, ___ and that's when I met you, yeah.

Coda 1

Chorus

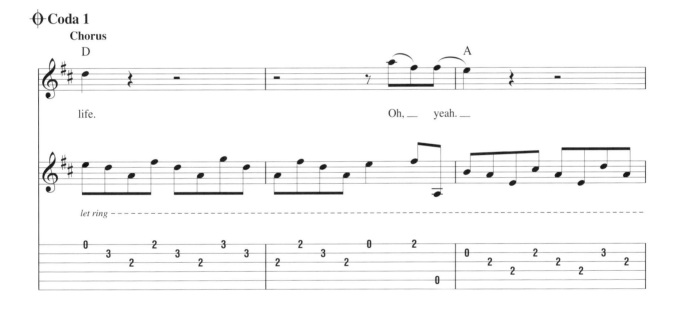

life.   Oh, ___ yeah. ___

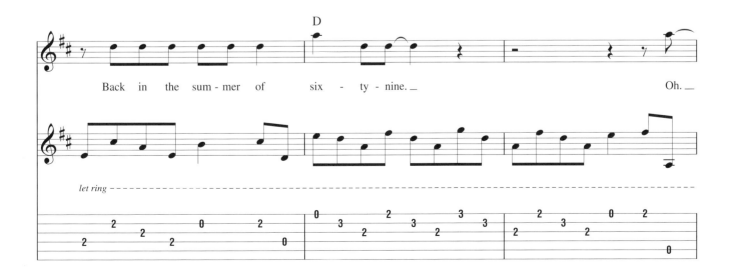

Back in the sum - mer of   six - ty - nine. ___   Oh. ___

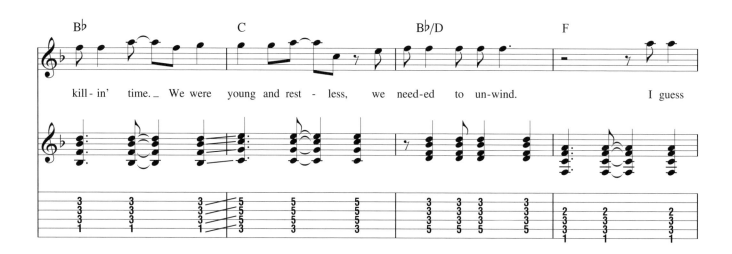

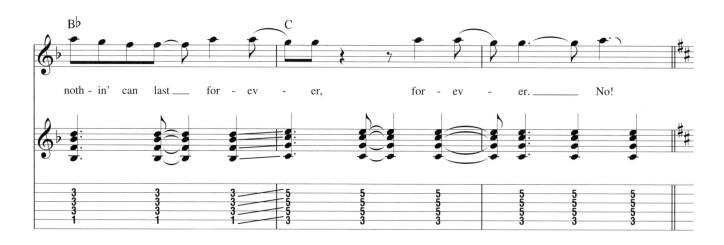

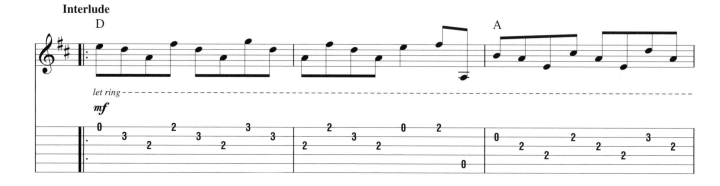

Verse

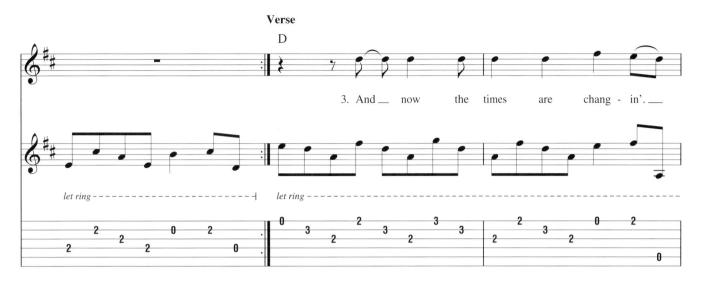

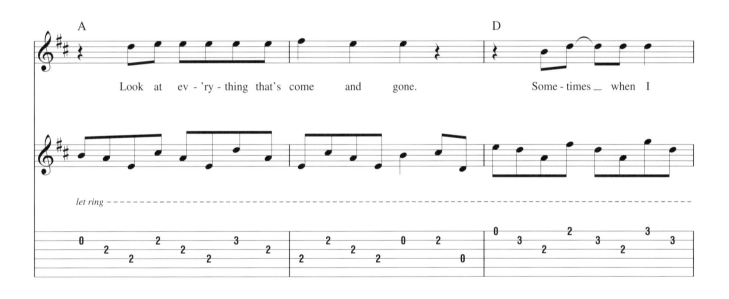

D.S. al Coda 2

Coda 2

life.   Oh, _____ yeah. _

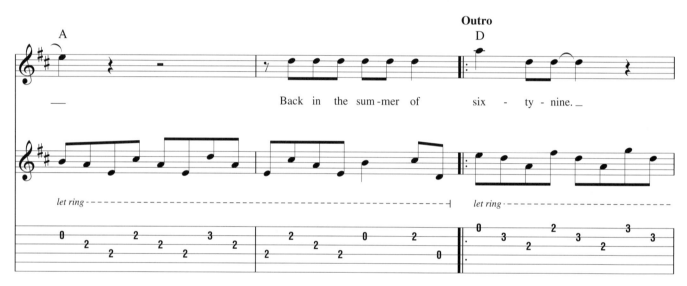

—   Back in the sum-mer of   six - ty - nine. _

Outro

Repeat and fade

Uh,   huh. _   It   was the sum-mer of

Additional Lyrics

Pre-Chorus 2., 3. Standin' on your mama's porch

You told me that { you'd wait / it'd last } forever.

Oh, and when you held my hand,
I knew that it was now or never.
Those were the best days of my life.

Sunshine of Your Love

Words and Music by Jack Bruce, Pete Brown and Eric Clapton

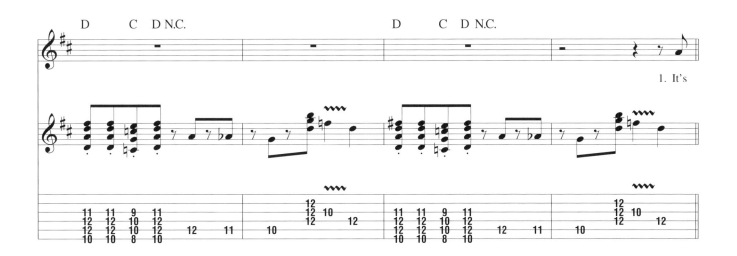

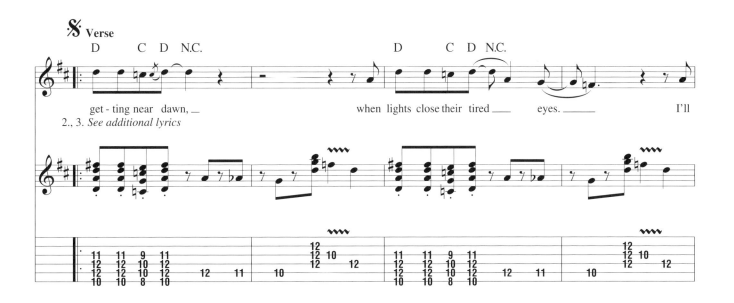

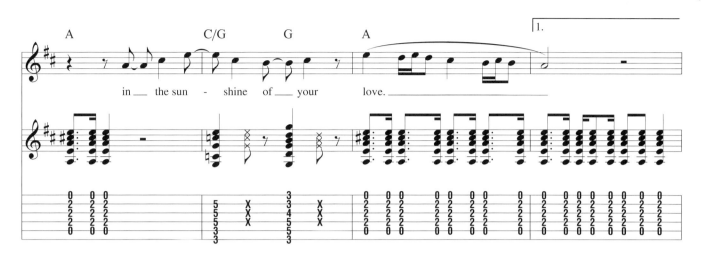

in ___ the sun - shine of ___ your love. _____

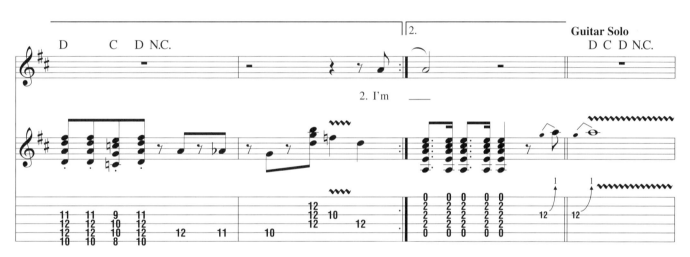

2. I'm ___

Guitar Solo

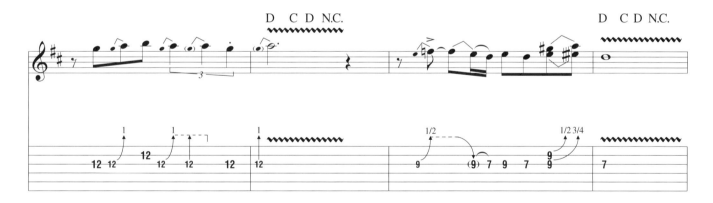

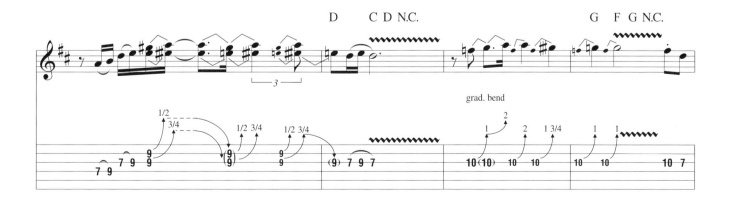

grad. bend

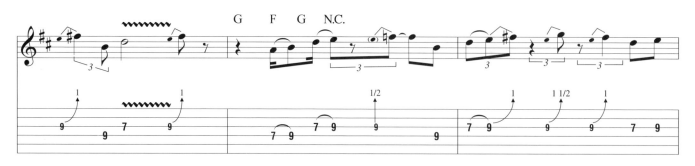

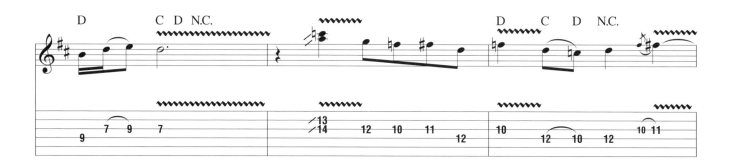

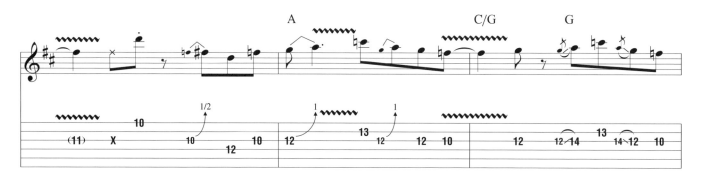

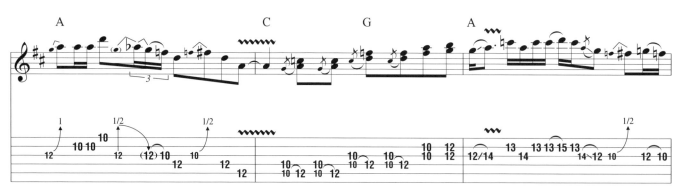

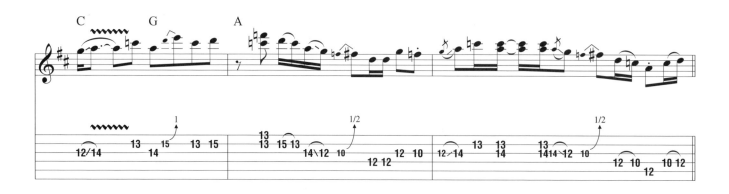

Additional Lyrics

I'm with you, my love;
The light shining through on you.
Yes, I'm with you, my love.
It's the morning and just we two.
I'll stay with you, darling, now.
I'll stay with you till my seeds are dried up.

Sweet Home Alabama

Words and Music by Ronnie Van Zant, Ed King and Gary Rossington

*Key signature denotes D Mixolydian.

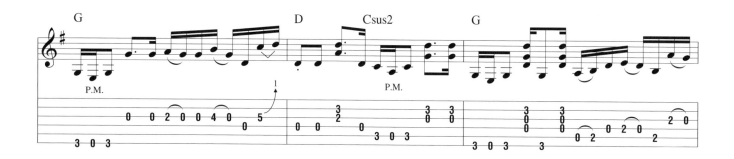

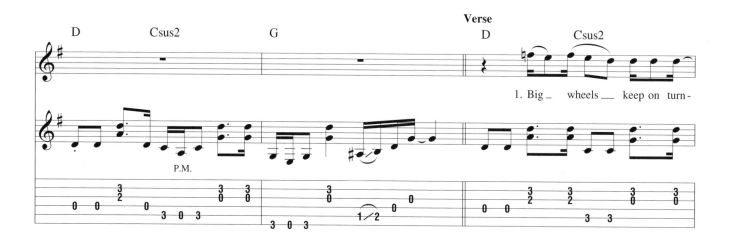

1. Big___ wheels___ keep on turn-

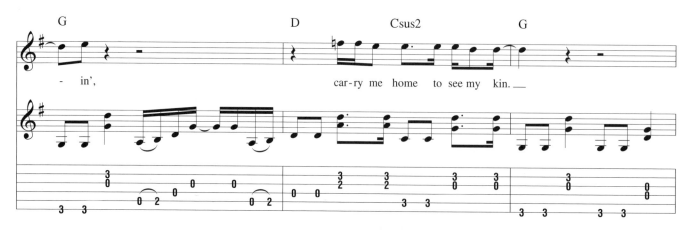

- in',   car-ry me home   to see my kin.___

Sing-in' songs a-bout _ the south - land.   I miss ole 'Bam - ee once a - gain _

Interlude

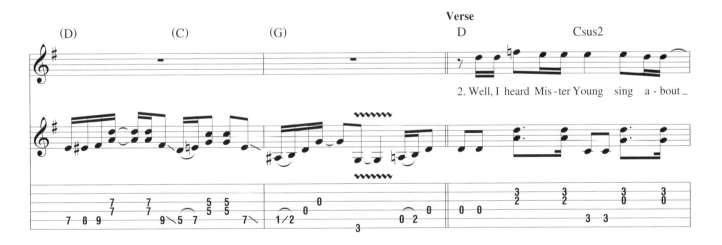

_ and I think it's a sin, _ yes.

Verse

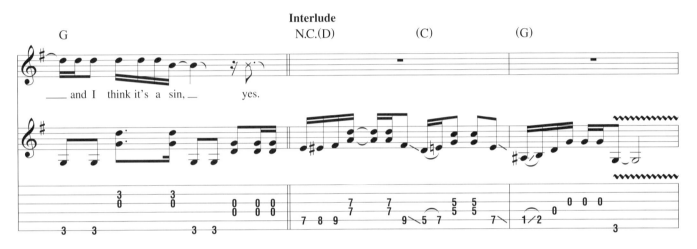

2. Well, I heard Mis-ter Young   sing   a - bout _

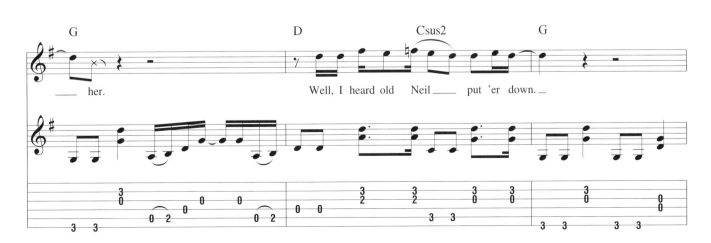

_ her.   Well, I heard old   Neil _ put 'er down. _

Well, I hope Neil Young will re-mem - ber,   a south-ern man _ don't need him a-

round,   an - y-how.   **Chorus**   Sweet _ home   Al - a - bam - a,

where the skies   are   so   blue. ___   Sweet _ home   Al - a-

bam - a,   Lord, I'm com-in' home   to   you.

Guitar Solo

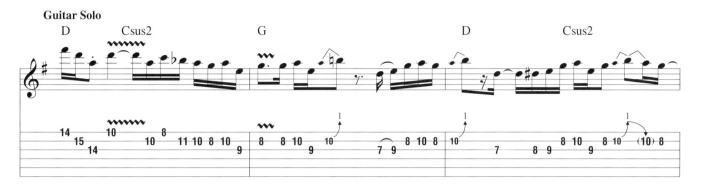

Verse

3. In Bir-ming - ham __ they love the gov - 'nor, boo, boo,

hoo. Now we all did __ what we could do. Now Wa-ter - gate __ does not

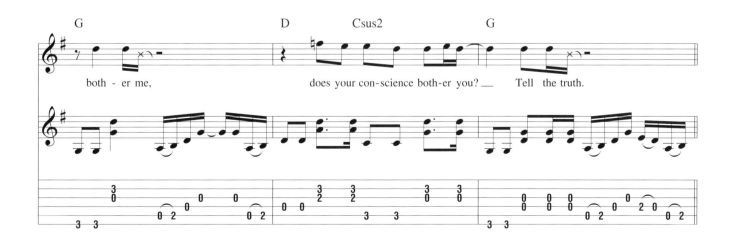

both - er me, does your con-science both-er you? __ Tell the truth.

Chorus

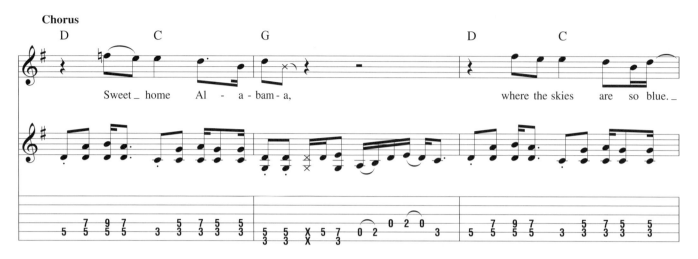

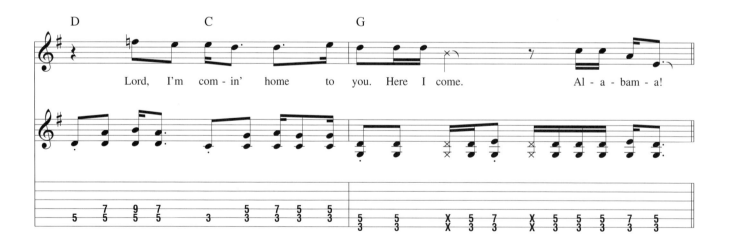

Guitar Solo

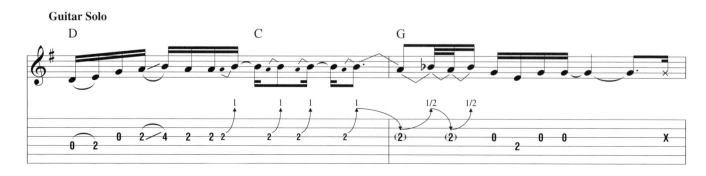

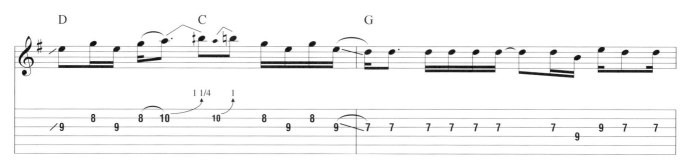

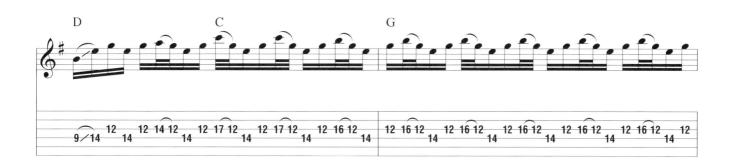

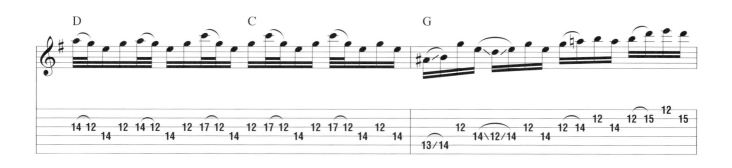

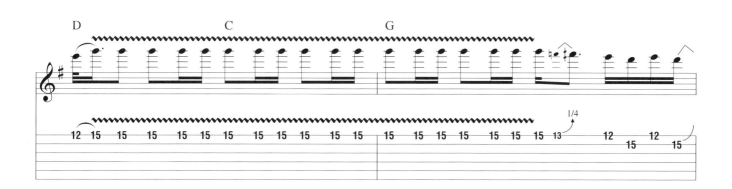

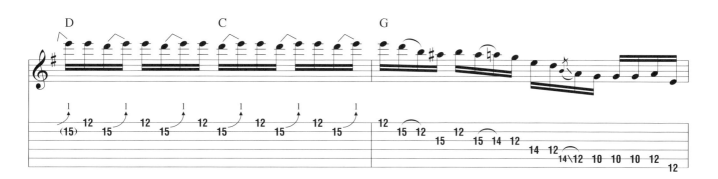

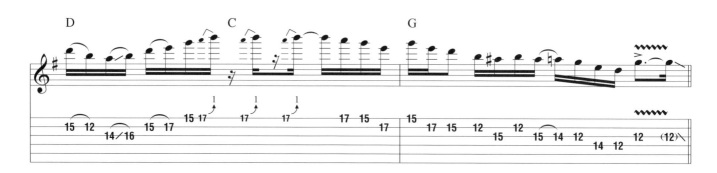

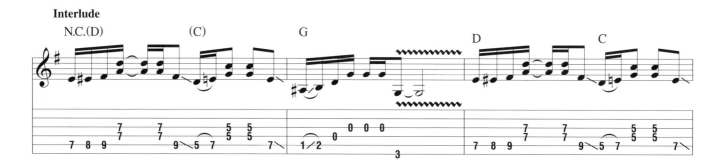

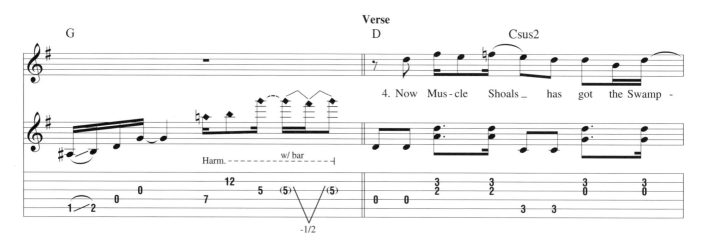

4. Now Mus-cle Shoals _ has got the Swamp-

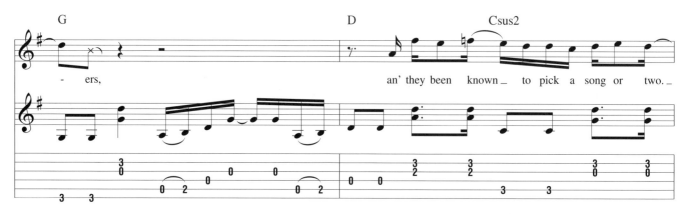

- ers,   an' they been known _ to pick a song or two. _

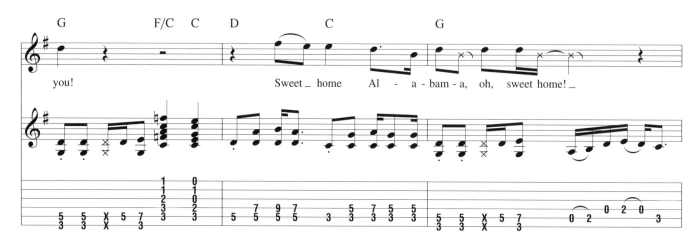

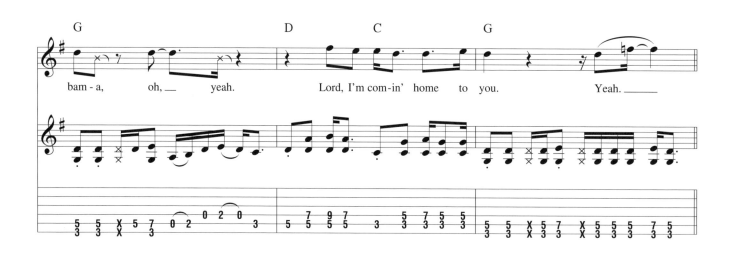

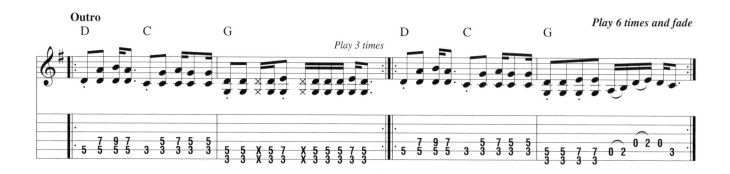

Takin' Care of Business

Words and Music by Randy Bachman

Intro
Moderate Rock ♩ = 126

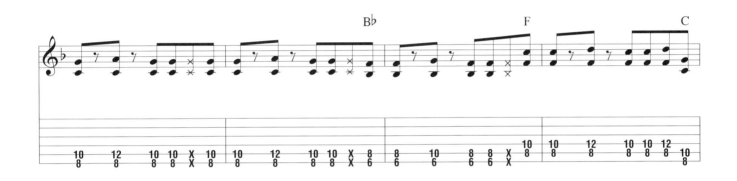

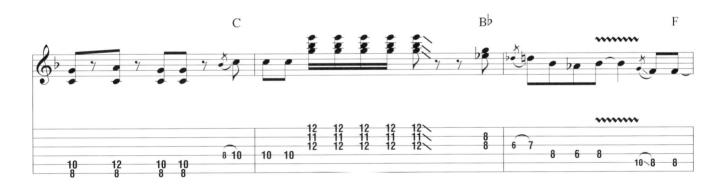

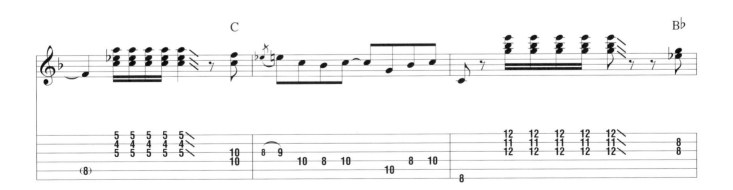

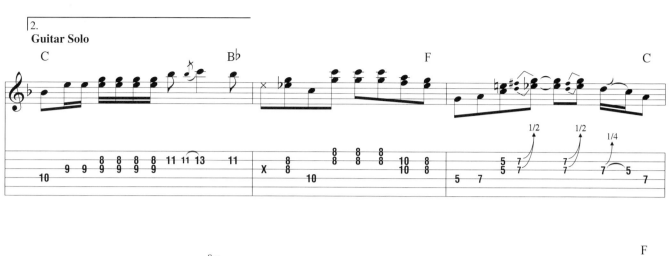

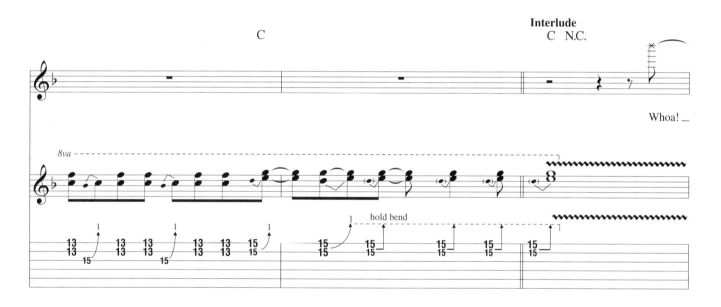

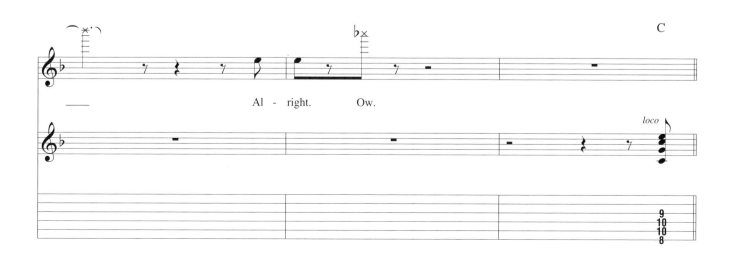

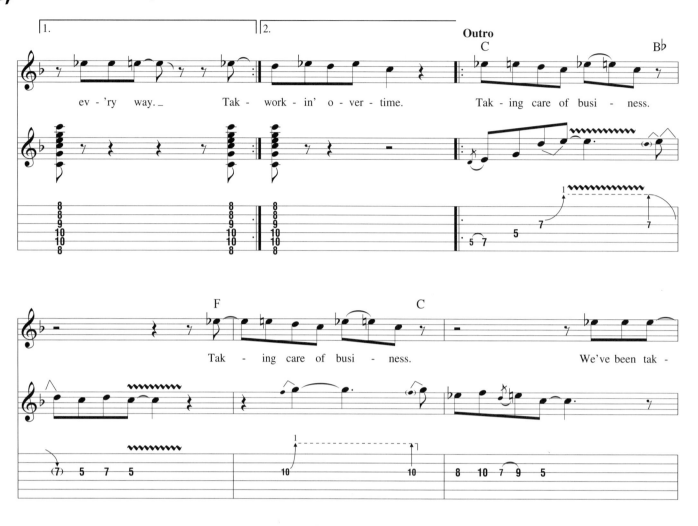

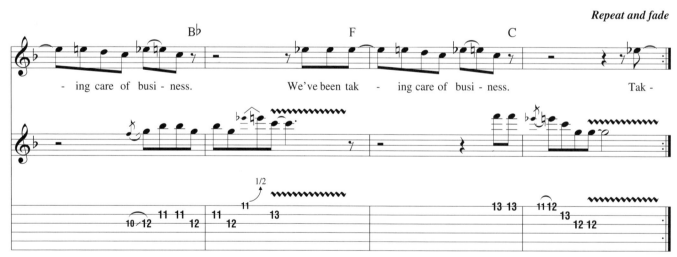

Additional Lyrics

2. There's work easy as fishin', you could be a musician,
   If you could make sounds loud or mellow.
   Get a second hand guitar, chances are you'll go far
   If you get in with the right group of fellows.
   People see you having fun just a lying in the sun.
   Tell them that you like it this way.
   It's the work that we avoid and we're all self employed.
   We love to work at nothing all day.
   And we've been...

Tush

Words and Music by Billy F Gibbons, Dusty Hill and Frank Beard

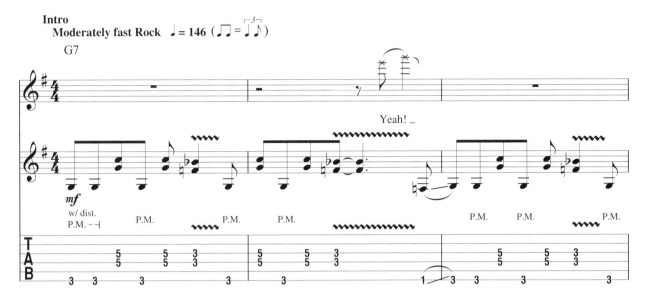

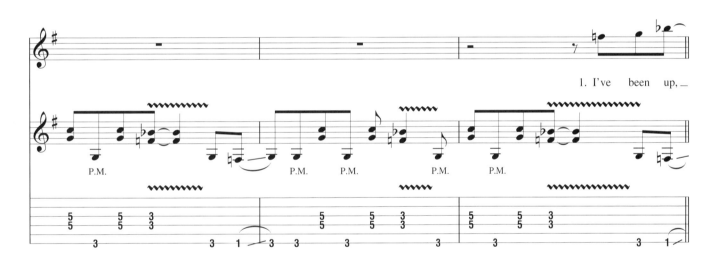

Guitar Solo

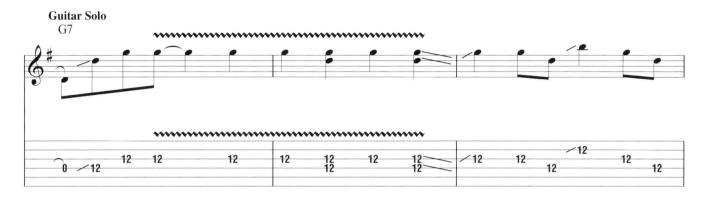

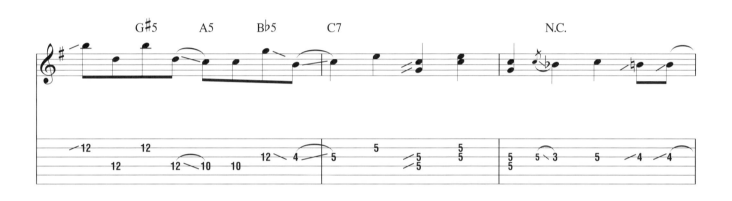

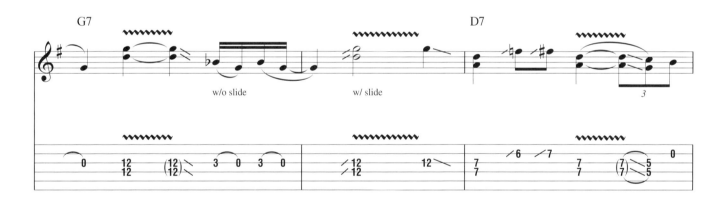

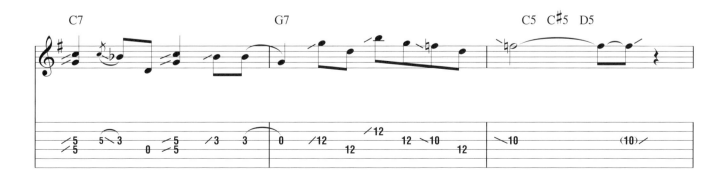

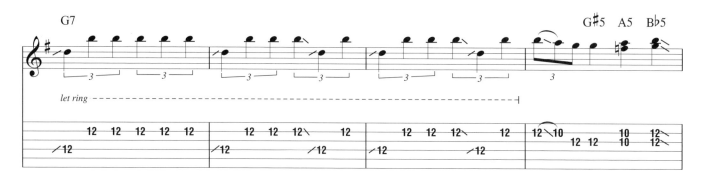

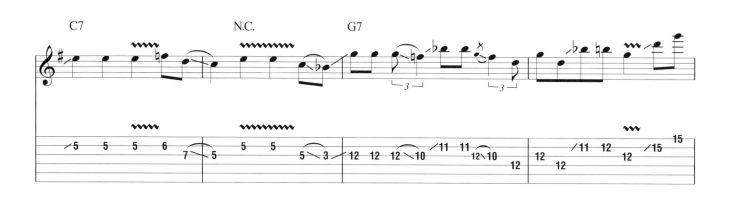

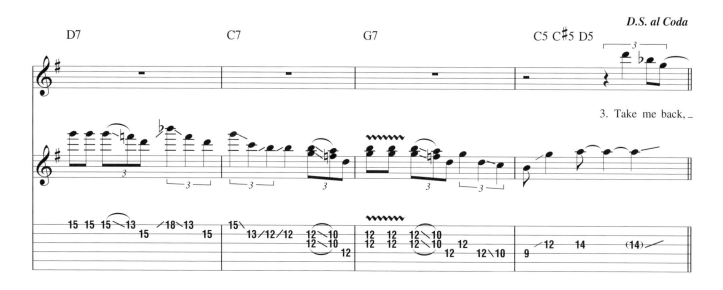

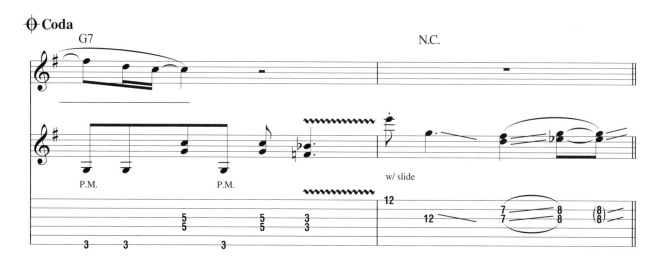

Outro-Guitar Solo

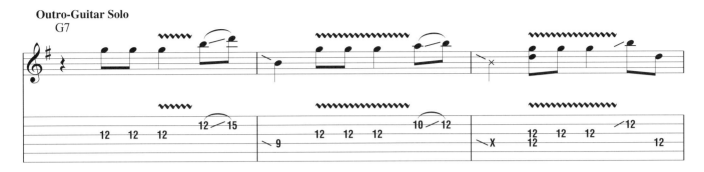

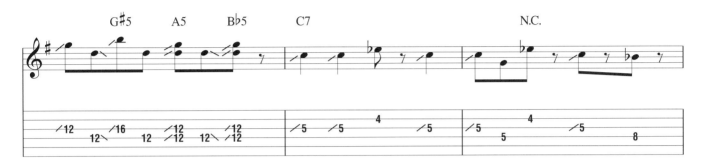

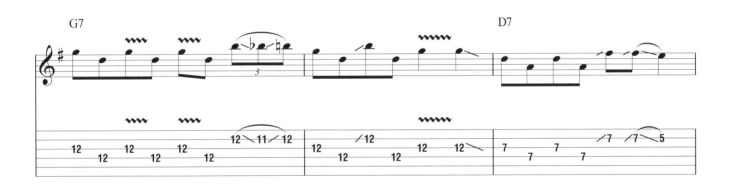

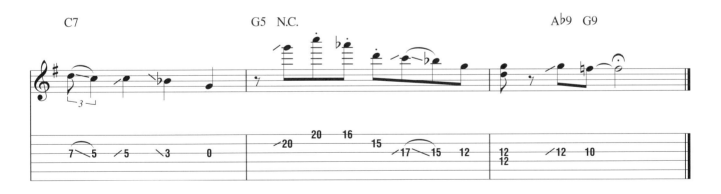

Additional Lyrics

2. I've been bad, I've been good,
   Dallas, Texas, Hollywood.
   I ain't askin' for much. Mm.
   I said, Lord, take me downtown.
   I'm just lookin' for some tush.

3. Take me back, way back home,
   Not by myself, not alone.
   I ain't askin' for much. Mm.
   I said, Lord, take me downtown.
   I'm just lookin' for some tush.

Walk Don't Run

By Johnny Smith

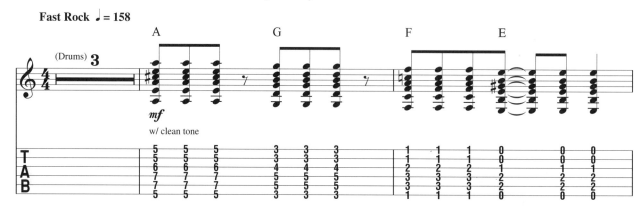

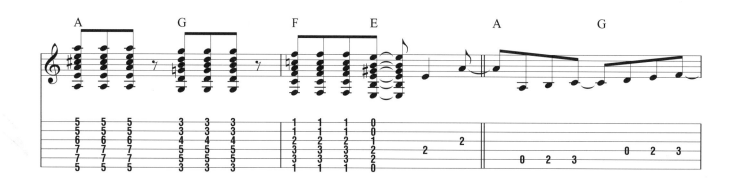

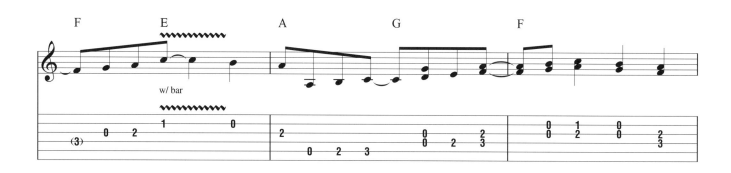

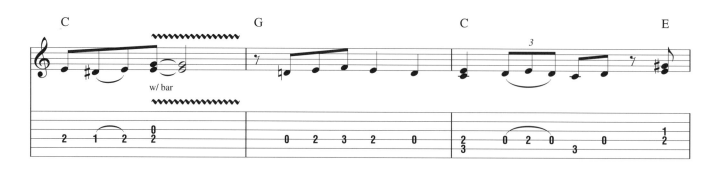

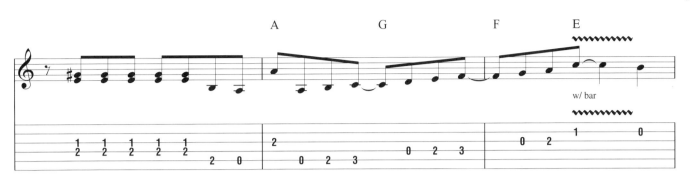

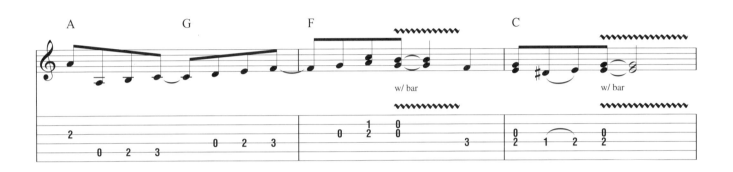

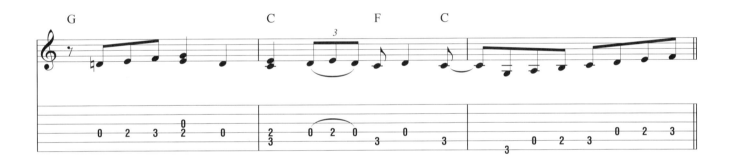

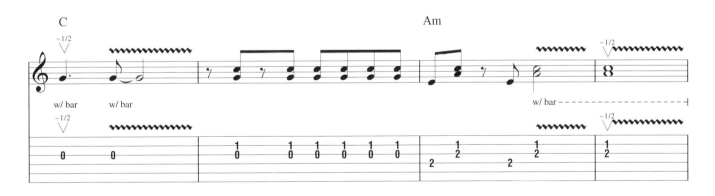

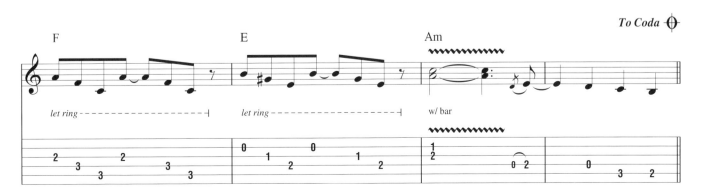

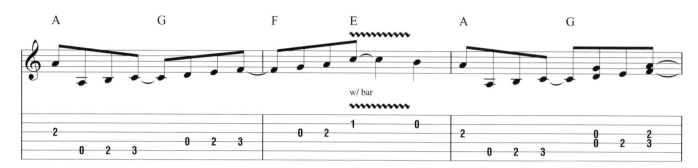

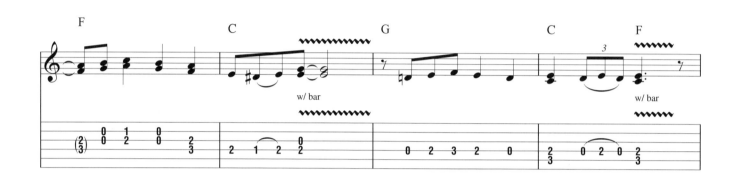

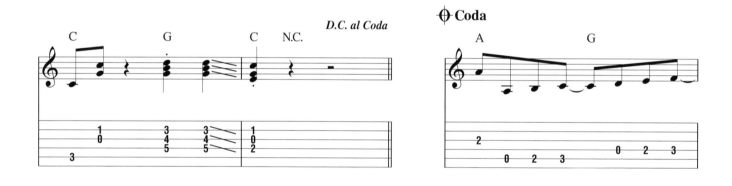

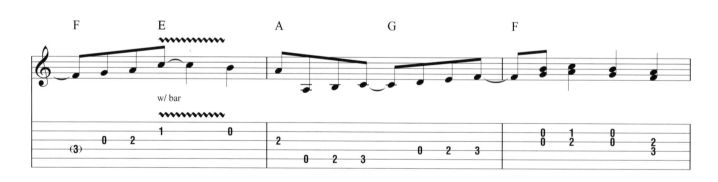

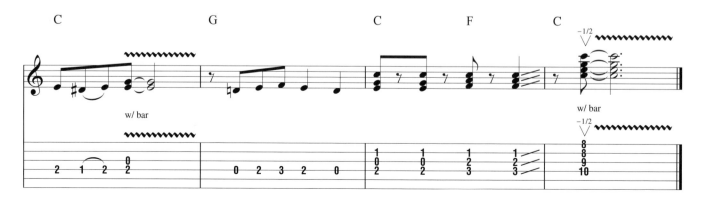

Walk This Way

Words and Music by Steven Tyler and Joe Perry

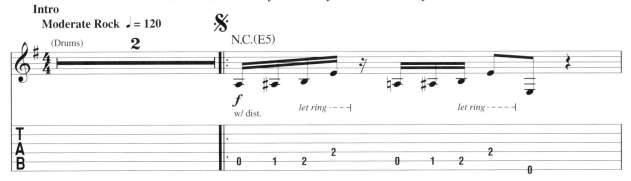

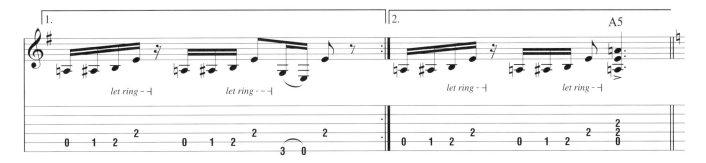

cheer - lead - er, was a real young bleed - er all the times I could rem - i - nisce, __ 'cause the

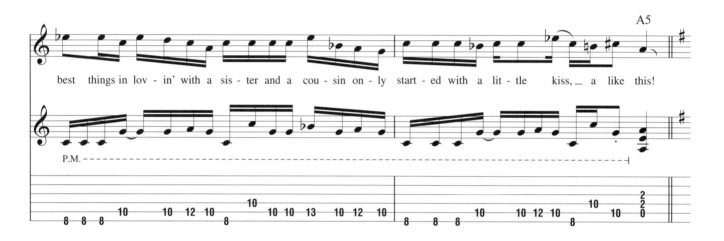

best things in lov - in' with a sis - ter and a cou - sin on - ly start - ed with a lit - tle   kiss, __ a like this!

Interlude
N.C.(E5)

Verse
N.C.(C7)

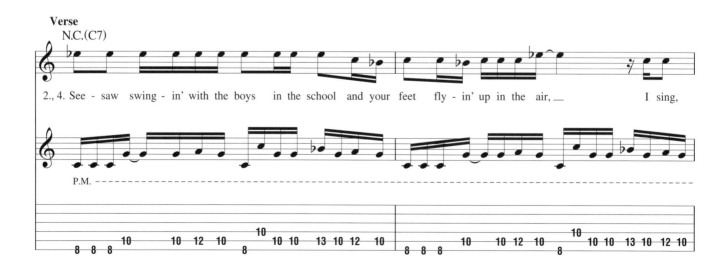

2., 4. See - saw swing - in' with the boys in the school and your feet fly - in' up in the air, __   I sing,

Guitar Solo

Like this!

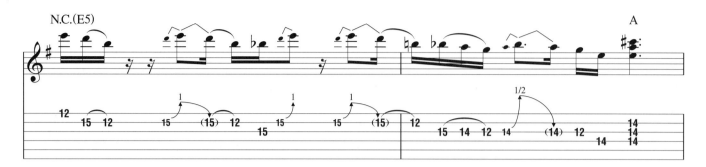

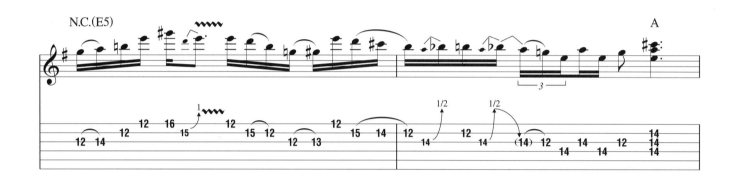

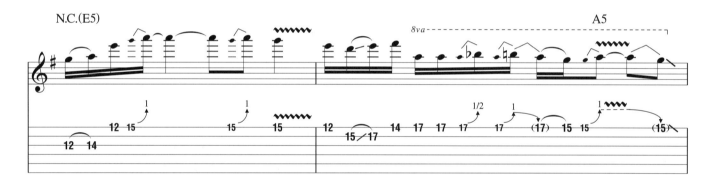

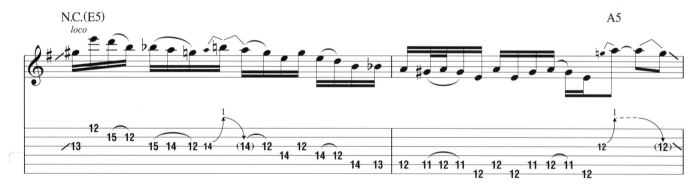

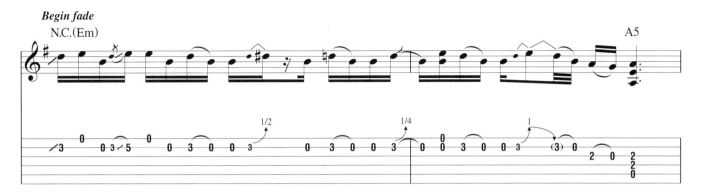

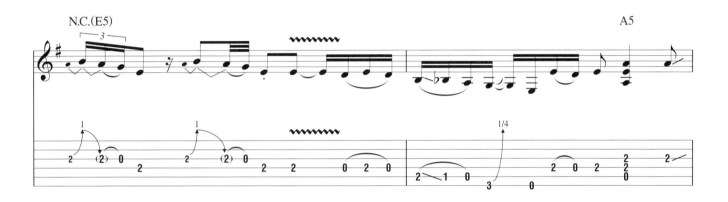

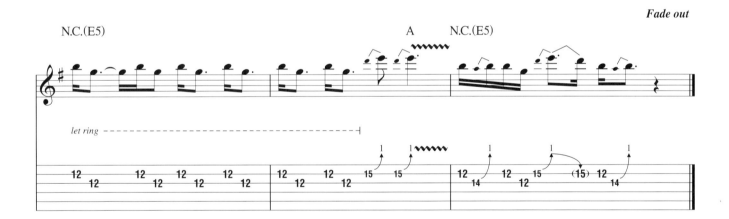

Additional Lyrics

3. School girl skinny with a classy kind a sassy little skirt's climbin' way up her knee,
   There was three young ladies in the school gym locker when I noticed they was lookin' at me.
   I was in high school loser, never made it with a lady till the boys told me somethin' I missed,
   Then my next door neighbor with a daughter had a favor so I gave her just a little kiss, a like this!

What I Like About You

Words and Music by Michael Skill, Wally Palamarchuk and James Marinos

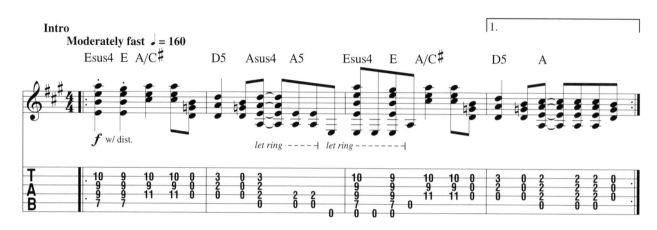

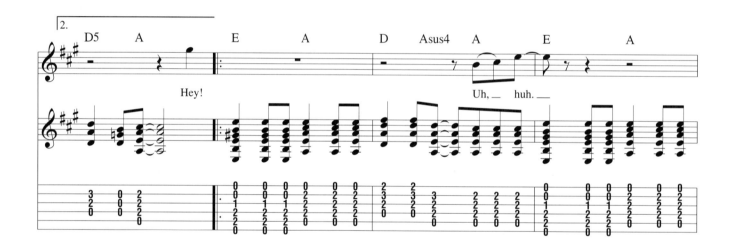

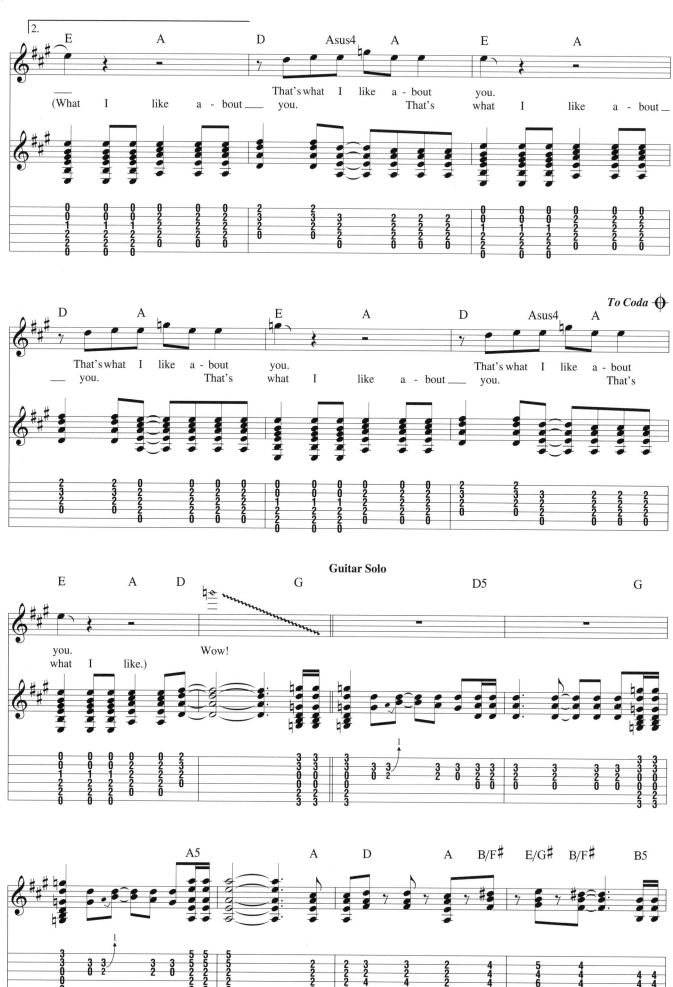

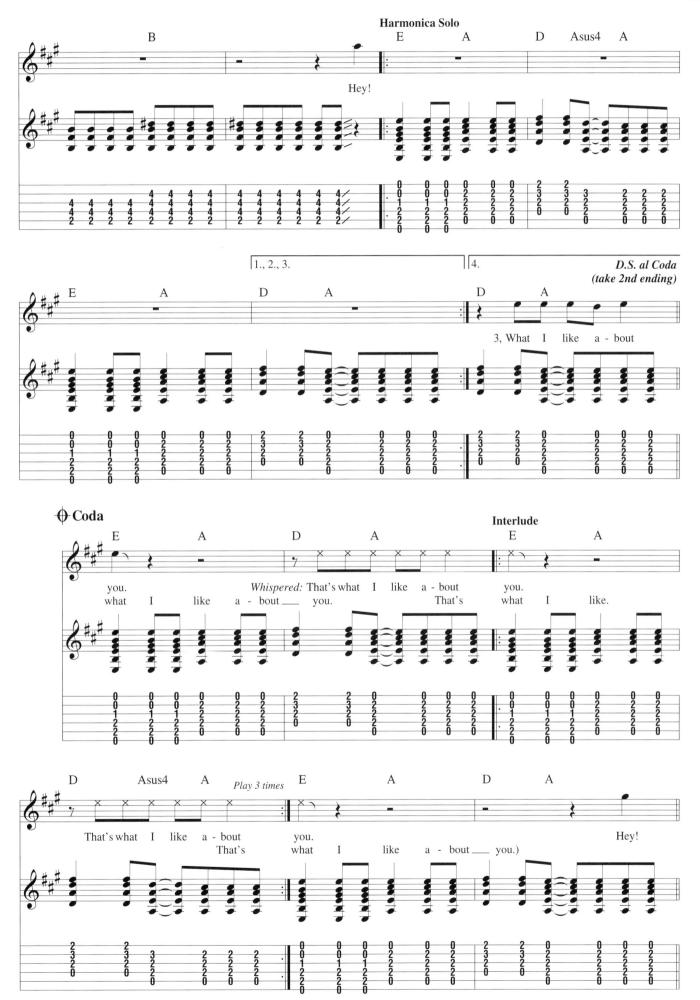

Outro

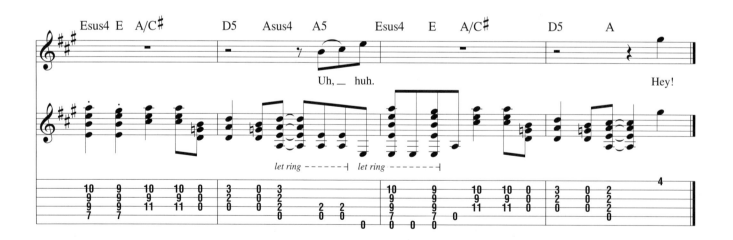

Additional Lyrics

2. What I like about you,
   You really know how to dance.
   When you go uptown jump around,
   Think about true romance. Yeah.

3. What I like about you,
   You keep me warm at night.
   Never wanna let you go,
   Know you make me feel alright. Yeah.

Wild Thing

Words and Music by Chip Taylor

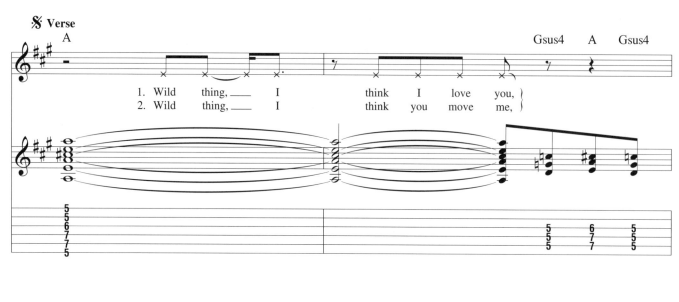

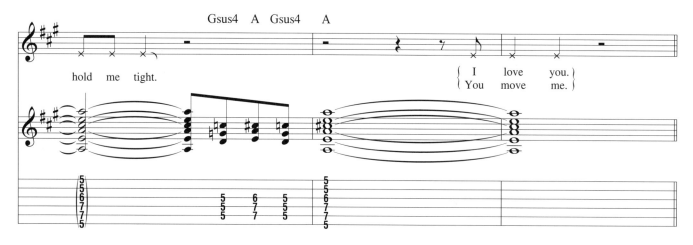

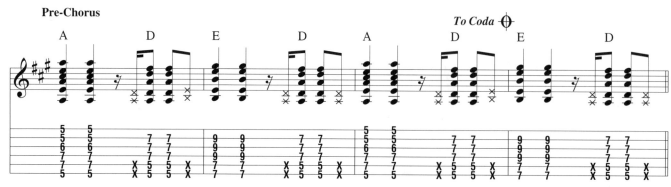

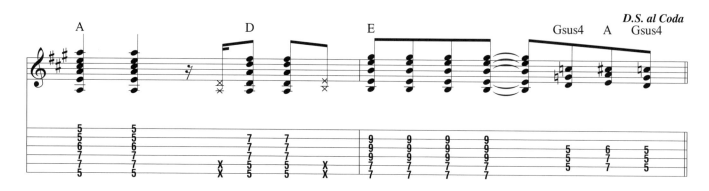

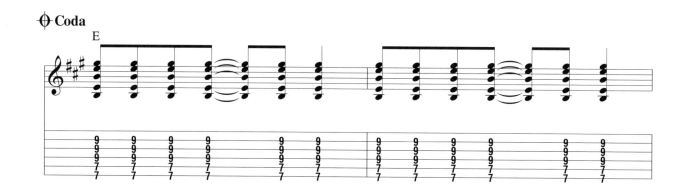

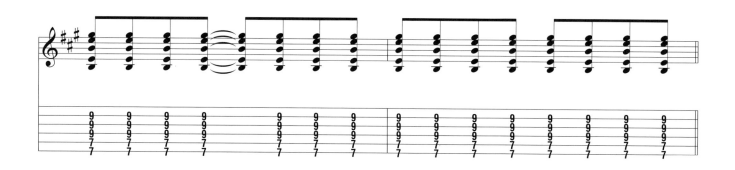

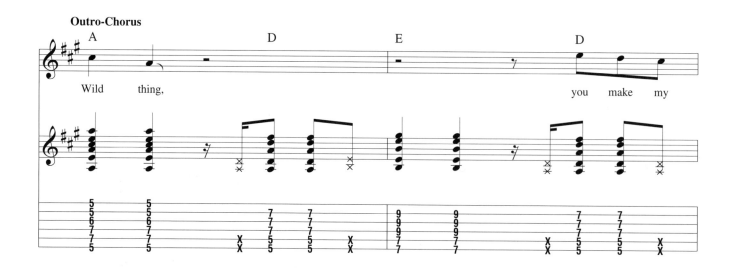

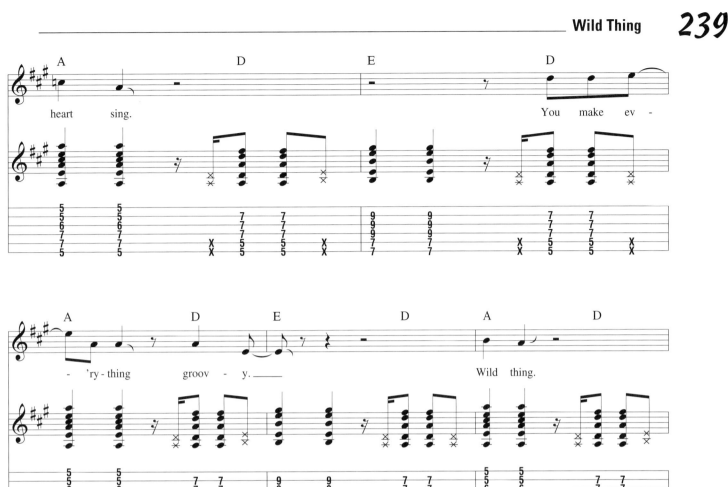

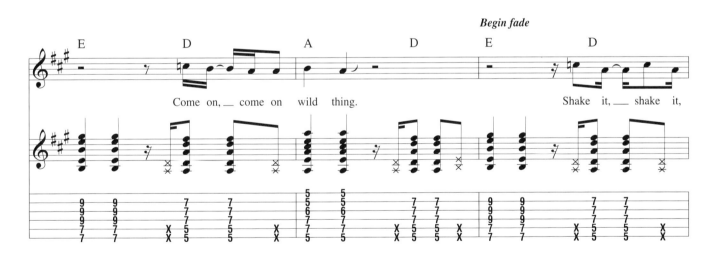

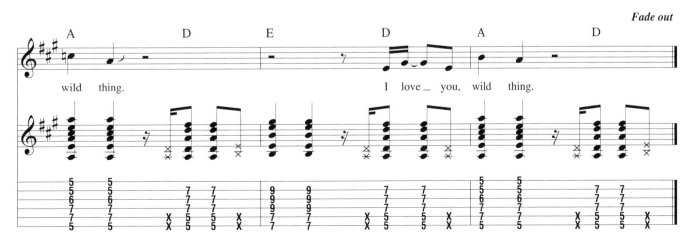

Won't Get Fooled Again

Words and Music by Pete Townshend

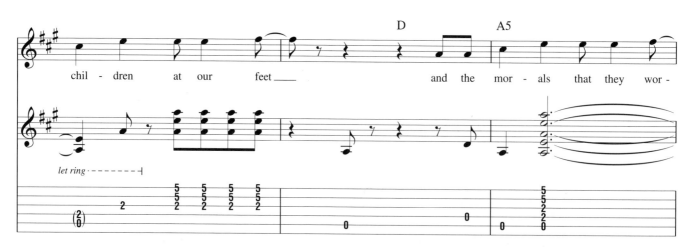

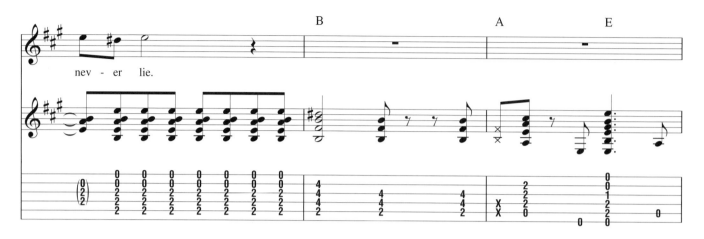

nev - er lie.

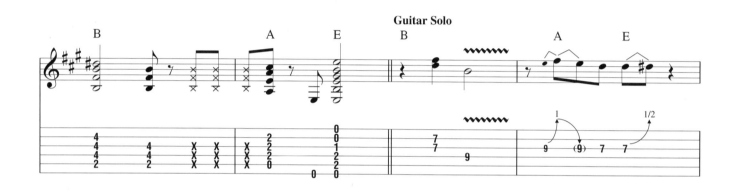

Guitar Solo

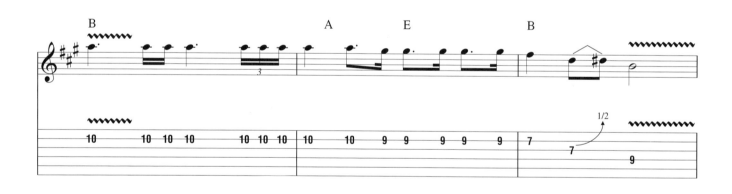

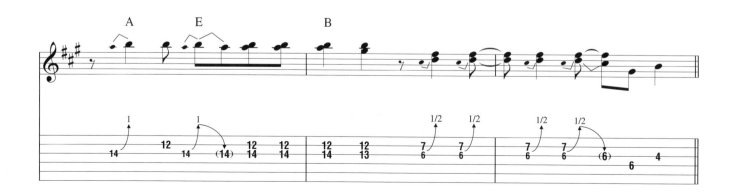

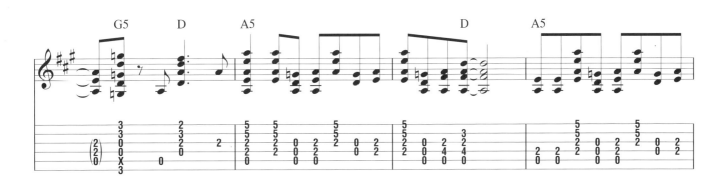

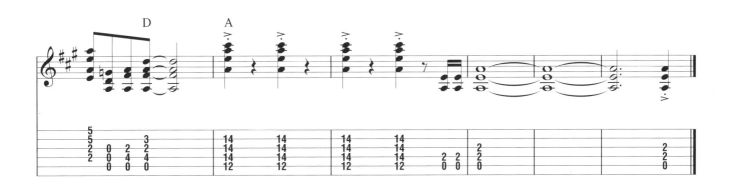

You Give Love a Bad Name

Words and Music by Jon Bon Jovi, Richie Sambora and Desmond Child

Intro

Moderate Rock ♩ = 123

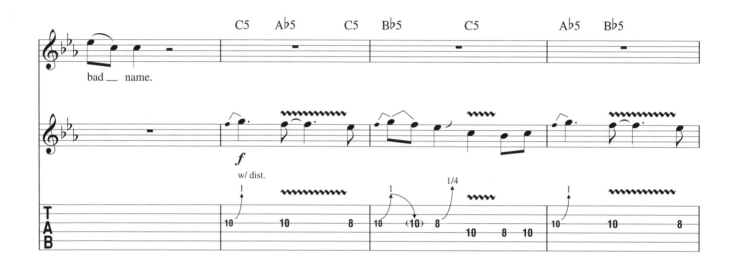

Shot through the heart   and you're to ___ blame, dar-lin', you give ___ love ___ a

bad ___ name.

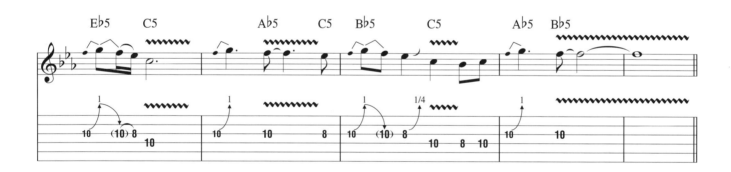

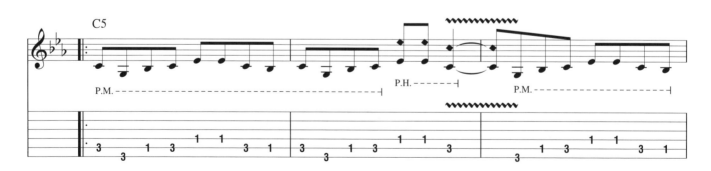

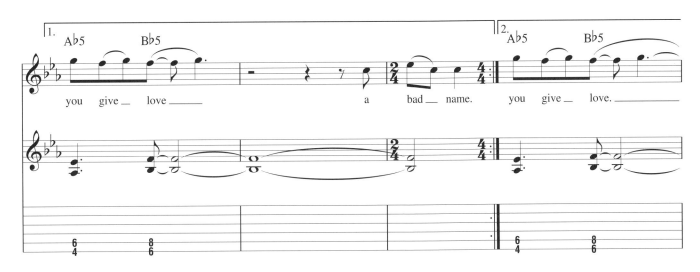

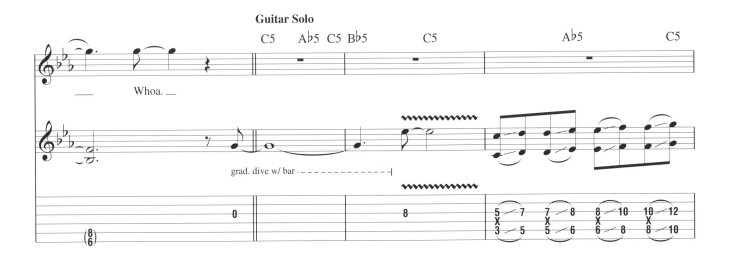

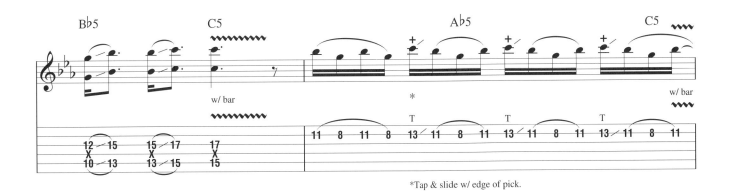

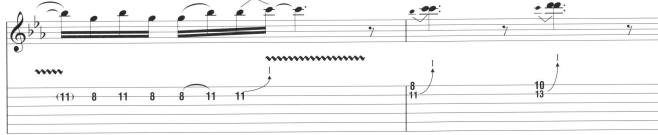

Breakdown-Chorus

Shot through the heart ___ and you're to ___ blame, you give love ___ a

bad ___ name. I play my part ___ and you play ___ your ___ game,

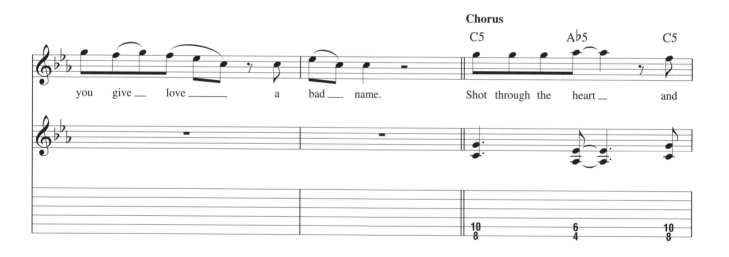

you give ___ love ___ a bad ___ name. Shot through the heart ___ and

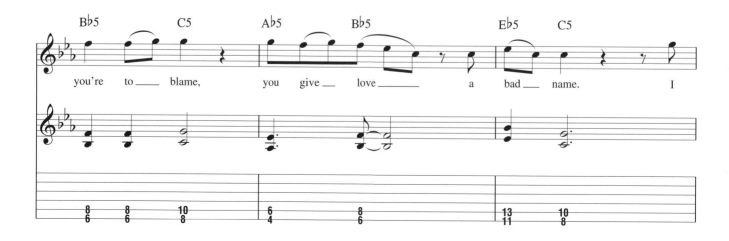

you're to ___ blame, you give ___ love ___ a bad ___ name. I

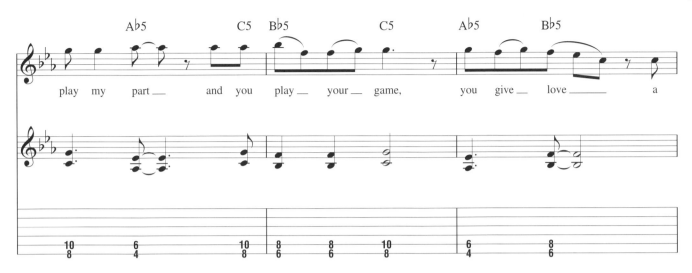

play my part ____ and you play ____ your ____ game, you give ____ love _____ a

Outro
w/ Voc. ad lib., till fade

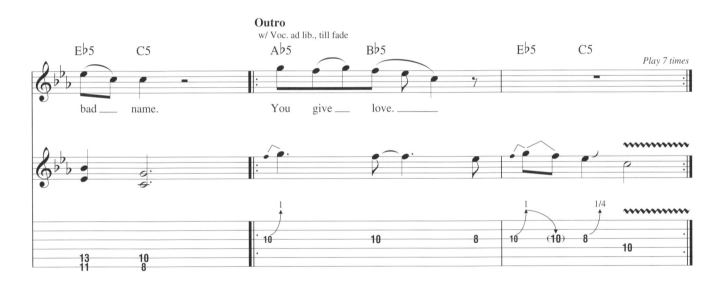

bad ____ name. You give ____ love. _____

Play 7 times

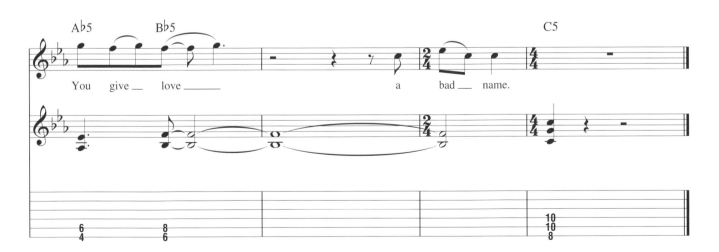

You give ____ love _____ a bad ____ name.

Additional Lyrics

2. You paint your smile on your lips.
   Blood-red nails on your fingertips.
   A school boy's dream, you act so shy.
   Your very first kiss was your first kiss goodbye.

Guitar Notation Legend

Guitar Music can be notated three different ways: on a *musical staff*, in *tablature*, and in *rhythm slashes*.

RHYTHM SLASHES are written above the staff. Strum chords in the rhythm indicated. Use the chord diagrams found at the top of the first page of the transcription for the appropriate chord voicings. Round noteheads indicate single notes.

THE MUSICAL STAFF shows pitches and rhythms and is divided by bar lines into measures. Pitches are named after the first seven letters of the alphabet.

TABLATURE graphically represents the guitar fingerboard. Each horizontal line represents a a string, and each number represents a fret.

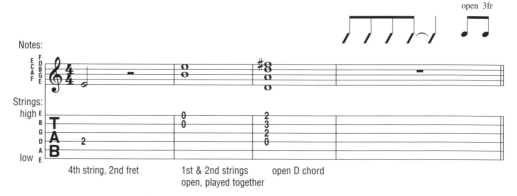

4th string, 2nd fret   1st & 2nd strings open, played together   open D chord

Definitions for Special Guitar Notation

HALF-STEP BEND: Strike the note and bend up 1/2 step.

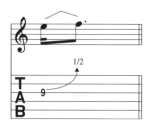

WHOLE-STEP BEND: Strike the note and bend up one step.

GRACE NOTE BEND: Strike the note and immediately bend up as indicated.

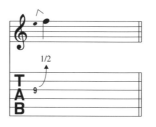

SLIGHT (MICROTONE) BEND: Strike the note and bend up 1/4 step.

BEND AND RELEASE: Strike the note and bend up as indicated, then release back to the original note. Only the first note is struck.

PRE-BEND: Bend the note as indicated, then strike it.

PRE-BEND AND RELEASE: Bend the note as indicated. Strike it and release the bend back to the original note.

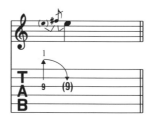

UNISON BEND: Strike the two notes simultaneously and bend the lower note up to the pitch of the higher.

VIBRATO: The string is vibrated by rapidly bending and releasing the note with the fretting hand.

WIDE VIBRATO: The pitch is varied to a greater degree by vibrating with the fretting hand.

HAMMER-ON: Strike the first (lower) note with one finger, then sound the higher note (on the same string) with another finger by fretting it without picking.

PULL-OFF: Place both fingers on the note to be sounded. Strike the first note without picking, pull the finger and the second (lower) note.

LEGATO SLIDE: Strike the first note and then slide the same fret-hand finger up or down to the second note. The second note is not struck.

SHIFT SLIDE: Same as legato slide, except the second note is struck.

TRILL: Very rapidly alternate between the notes indicated by continuously hammering on and pulling off.

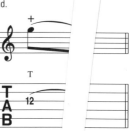

TAPPING: Hammer ("tap") the fret indicated with the pick-hand index or middle finger and pull off to the note fretted by the fret hand.

NATURAL HARMONIC: Strike the note while the fret-hand lightly touches the string directly over the fret indicated.

Harm.

PINCH HARMONIC: The note is fretted normally and a harmonic is produced by adding the edge of the thumb or the tip of the index finger of the pick hand to the normal pick attack.

P.H.

HARP HARMONIC: The note is fretted normally and a harmonic is produced by gently resting the pick hand's index finger directly above the indicated fret (in parentheses) while the pick hand's thumb or pick assists by plucking the appropriate string.

H.H.

PICK SCRAPE: The edge of the pick is rubbed down (or up) the string, producing a scratchy sound.

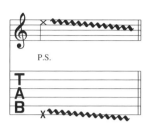

P.S.

MUFFLED STRINGS: A percussive sound is produced by laying the fret hand across the string(s) without depressing, and striking them with the pick hand.

PALM MUTING: The note is partially muted by the pick hand lightly touching the string(s) just before the bridge.

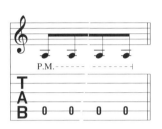

P.M.

RAKE: Drag the pick across the strings indicated with a single motion.

rake

TREMOLO PICKING: The note is picked as rapidly and continuously as possible.

ARPEGGIATE: Play the notes of the chord indicated by quickly rolling them from bottom to top.

VIBRATO BAR DIVE AND RETURN: The pitch of the note or chord is dropped a specified number of steps (in rhythm) then returned to the original pitch.

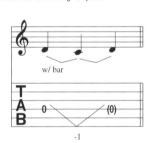

w/ bar

VIBRATO BAR SCOOP: Depress the bar just before striking the note, then quickly release the bar.

w/ bar

VIBRATO BAR DIP: Strike the note and then immediately drop a specified number of steps, then release back to the original pitch.

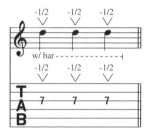

w/ bar

Additional Musical Definitions

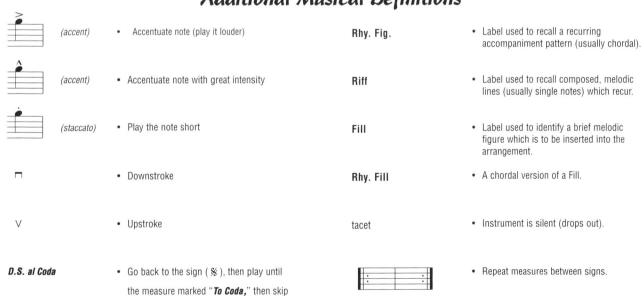

(accent)	• Accentuate note (play it louder)	**Rhy. Fig.**	• Label used to recall a recurring accompaniment pattern (usually chordal).
(accent)	• Accentuate note with great intensity	**Riff**	• Label used to recall composed, melodic lines (usually single notes) which recur.
(staccato)	• Play the note short	**Fill**	• Label used to identify a brief melodic figure which is to be inserted into the arrangement.
	• Downstroke	**Rhy. Fill**	• A chordal version of a Fill.
V	• Upstroke	tacet	• Instrument is silent (drops out).

D.S. al Coda • Go back to the sign (𝄋), then play until the measure marked "**To Coda**," then skip to the section labelled "**Coda**."

• Repeat measures between signs.

D.C. al Fine • Go back to the beginning of the song and play until the measure marked "**Fine**" (end).

1. 2. • When a repeated section has different endings, play the first ending only the first time and the second ending only the second time.

NOTE: Tablature numbers in parentheses mean:
1. The note is being sustained over a system (note in standard notation is tied), or
2. The note is sustained, but a new articulation (such as a hammer-on, pull-off, slide or vibrato begins), or
3. The note is a barely audible "ghost" note (note in standard notation is also in parentheses).

Chord Chart

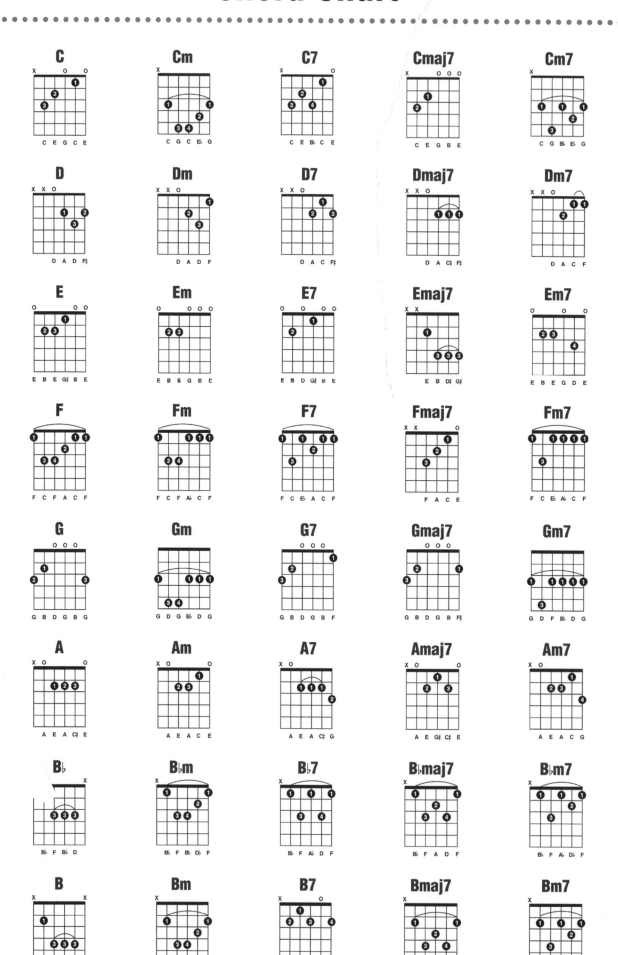